The Last Beach Boy

A True American Story

Of Life and Adventure

Robert (Bobby) Solano

With Victor DiGenti

Dreams

When you find a dream
inside your heart
don't ever let it go …
For dreams
Are the tiny seeds
From which tomorrows grow

Bobby was born a Solano, part of the oldest family in the oldest city in America — St. Augustine, Florida. Come read and enjoy the adventure.

ISBN: 979-8-9870581-0-7

Printed and published in the United States of America by
Windrusher Hall Press
P. O. Box 1587
Ponte Vedra Beach, FL 32004

Windrusher Hall Press

CONTENTS

PART THREE – HIGH SCHOOL DAYS

PART FIVE – THE SOLANO FAMILY

PART SIX – LIFE IS A FEAST

DEDICATION

This book is dedicated to my son Robert "Bucky" Solano and my grandson Jacob Solano. Terrible accidents claimed the lives of both boys at an early age—Bucky was only twelve years old when he died and Jacob was seventeen. They were fine young men who would have helped make the world a better place. They were positive and strong. We miss them and will never forget them.

My son David Solano lost his battle with a deadly disease but gave our family a lot of joy and happiness while he was with us. David was an unbelievably motivated young man throughout the young years of his life.

I also dedicate this book to the rest of my family, whom I love so much—my sons Danny, Britt, Brian, and my lovely daughter Kimberly. I have a wonderful bunch of grandchildren and a couple of great grandchildren. Please see the list of the important people in my life in the section I call the "Cast of Characters."

I also want to recognize my many friends during my younger years, including the guys on our high school state championship basketball team, especially our great cheerleaders and the entire 1954 graduating class of Fletcher High School in Jacksonville Beach, Florida.

You'll meet some of them in this book, and I wish I could tell you about all of the others, but that would take forever. Maybe in another book.

Thanks also to Wendy, Brian, Kimberly, and everyone who helped make this book possible.

God, grant me the serenity to accept
the things I cannot change,
courage to change the things I can,
and wisdom to know the difference.
The Serenity Prayer

"The price of success is hard work, dedication to the job
at hand, and the determination that whether we win or
lose, we have applied the best of ourselves
to the task at hand."
~Vince Lombardi

PREFACE
Running Shine

I'd heard the story countless times before, but each time seemed like the first. We were sitting around the fire at our hunting camp at Twelve Mile Swamp, and Pop (Tola) and the others were swapping stories and sipping whiskey. I hung on every word as Pop spun the tale of how he and my father, Ally, ran moonshine for Pop's father. The story crackled with adventure, danger, and even a little sex. What boy wouldn't be captivated hearing such rousing details about a father he barely knew? Here's the story as Pop told us over the flickering flames so many years ago.

There's no doubt the waitress was a pretty young thing, and my father, Albert "Ally" Solano, was doing his best to keep her entertained. Both elbows on the counter, he leaned into his conversation like a pitcher on the mound preparing to deliver his best curve ball. Seventeen-year-old Ally, confident in his good looks and silver tongue, was in the middle of his sales pitch when Bartola "Tola" Pacetti burst through the North Carolina truck stop door and hustled up to my father.

"Ally," Tola said, grabbing Ally's shoulder and rudely interrupting his conversation with the waitress. He whispered urgently in my father's ear. "We got to get the hell out of here fast. I'll explain in the truck. Let's go."

Ally turned to the waitress he'd been charming and, with his best smile, said, "I'll be back, honey. Keep the coffee warm."

Once outside the truck stop, Ally said, "What the hell is going on Tola?"

"The Feds are on to us, so get your ass moving. They've already stopped the

Chicago buyer's truck."

"How do you know?" my father asked him.

Tola said he'd called his father, Camilo, on the pay phone outside the truck stop while Ally, my dad, was making moves on the waitress. "He was tipped off about the Feds and warned us before we were stopped. He didn't know who ratted us out, but he thinks another buyer from up north squealed because they wanted the shipment."

Tola now had Ally's full attention, and they ran to the old Model T parked out front. Tola slipped behind the wheel and cranked her up. He gripped the wheel so hard that his knuckles were white. He scanned the parking lot, took a deep breath, and turned to his partner, obviously upset.

"You know, I was working to save our butts while you in there working on that little waitress."

Ally brushed it off, saying, "Tola, you never know what piece of information that little girl might have that could help us."

"Yeah, I know what kind of piece you were working on."

Ally could only laugh.

A large black sedan pulled in and parked ss they exited the truck stop. Tola stomped on the gas as soon as they were out of sight. They both figured the black sedan belonged to the Feds and began searching for a place to hide the truck. No way could they outrun them in their old Ford.

"There, Tola, turn in," my father yelled, pointing to a dirt road to their left. Tola swerved onto the dirt road, drove a few hundred feet, and squeezed the truck behind a clump of bushes. He cut the engine and the lights, and they got out and waited.

Pop was into his story now, telling us they held their breath as a vehicle approached, but it was only a pickup truck. Pop said a car came barreling down the highway a minute later. It was the black sedan, and it sped right by them.

Pop admitted they were both scared, but my dad said, "Let me drive, Tola. I think I know where we can hide, but we gotta get out of here now."

Ally took the wheel and returned to the country road, driving in the opposite direction of the speeding black sedan. "Keep an eye out behind us, Tola," he said.

Pop said they were going pretty fast when my father put on the brakes and pulled in behind the truck stop they had just left. "What the hell you doing, Ally?"

"Just stay calm, Tola. I'll be right back."

But Tola wasn't in the mood to stay calm. "Ally, you crazy bastard, you going to get us caught."

Ally jumped out of the truck and disappeared through the restaurant's back door. In a few minutes, he came out with a bag in his hand, climbed behind the wheel, slammed the truck in gear, and eased back out on the highway.

"Ally, what the hell did you do? And what's in the bag?"

"That's the hamburgers we had ordered. I was hungry, and I didn't want that little girl to have to pay for them if we didn't come back."

"Ally, you are a damn trip. Here you are thinking about food and that *piece* of information when we could be close to going to prison. Don't you know the Feds are on our ass? But don't worry because if they catch us, I understand they feed you before putting you on the chain gang."

"Tola, they ain't going to catch us, not tonight anyways. Just shut up and watch for Plum Street, it will be on your side."

Tola was confused. "Do you mind telling me where the hell you taking us?"

"Not at all but keep looking for that street while we talking. My piece of information little waitress friend said we could hang out at her place till tomorrow if we wanted to. Now don't you think you owe me an apology saying I was not on the job when I just got us a hideout? Quit worrying and bitching so much and look for the damn street."

They found Plum Street, but Tola didn't believe a word my father was saying. "You are telling me the biggest lie of your life, Ally. Admit it."

When Pop told us this story, he said Ally started laughing and stopped in front of a little cottage. With a look of satisfaction, he turned to Tola and said, "The waitress told me she left a light on every night. Tonight, she left it on for us, but mainly for me." And this is when he laughed again before sharing more of his conversation with the waitress.

"Mary is our little savior's name, and she said to pull the truck behind the cottage and make ourselves at home. She gets off at midnight, but she is sorry she only has one bed and a couch. So, I guess I will have to sleep in the bed with her and you can have the couch."

Pop was still skeptical, but my father was in a good mood, telling him, "You know me, Tola. I am always willing to go that extra mile for us and do what I have to do. Regardless."

Laughing like hell while hitting Ally on the arm, Pop said, "Ally, God's going to get you for lying so much." But sure enough, as Pop related the story, "That damn Ally character ended up sleeping with Mary, and I slept on the couch. But we were blessed for her help, and I was glad to be on that couch and not on a hard bunk in some damn jail in North Carolina."

Pop said, "Mary was a sweetheart and she probably saved us from getting caught. We stayed inside her cottage for the next two days except when she took us to town in her car and we bought a bunch of groceries for her before she went to work."

While staying at Mary's cottage, Tola called his dad, Camilo, and let him know they were okay and safe for now. His dad told him they should stay put until he got another delivery order for the shine they had in the truck. He wanted it sold, not brought back to Florida, saying it would be safer than trying to make it back to Florida and crossing state borders with a load of shine.

On the third day, Camilo called with new delivery instructions. They were to head south on US 17 out of Wilmington for about three miles, look for a little garage and Texaco gas station with two hand gas pumps outside. There they should ask for Joe and speak only to Joe. With their new delivery destination, they thanked Mary for all her help and gave her some money, though she didn't want to take it.

After they said goodbye to Mary and headed south, Ally said, "Well, Tola, at least we are headed towards home, but I was kinda hoping we were going to have to stay a couple more nights at Mary's."

Tola said, "Yeah, I wonder why?"

Sure enough, they soon spotted the Texaco station and parked at the pumps. A little guy in overalls came out, wiping his hands on a greasy rag. "What grade of gas you want, fellows?" he asked.

"We want to talk to Joe. Is he here?" Tola said.

"Yes, he sure the hell is. That's me." Then Joe saw our Florida license plate and said, "You must be the fellas from Florida with a load of boxes for me."

Tola said, "Yes, and you got a package for us."

"Sure enough do. Back up to that garage door and we'll unload your boxes to the back of the garage."

Before Tola could put the truck in gear, a sheriff's car drove up to the other side of the gas pumps. Pop said it felt like his heart stopped, thinking, *Oh, shit, this is it. They got us.*

The deputy leaned out, called Joe by name, and said a car was out of gas back up the road about a mile and wanted to know if he could help them. Joe said, "Sure, Mac, I'll call the wife and ask her to look after the station while I run up there with some gas. It'll be just a few minutes."

The deputy thanked him and said he'd drive back and stay with the car until Joe arrived. After the deputy left, they looked at each other, and no one spoke for what seemed like forever. Then Ally said, "Joe, where is your bathroom? I got to go check my pants."

This broke the tension, and they all laughed. In ten minutes, they unloaded the shine, gassed up, and headed south toward home.

***

I heard this story and others every hunting season at the Twelve Mile Swamp hunting camp in St. Augustine but could never listen to them enough. All the men would laugh and have another shot of shine or red whiskey. Tola and my father, Albert Solano, Jr. (known to family and friends as Ally or Buck), had been friends a long time, attending school together in St. Augustine, though only through the sixth grade.

Pop and Ally ran moonshine for Pop's father, Camilo, usually on the weekends. They were only teenagers then, and Pop said they made good money running shine, but that last adventure in North Carolina scared the daylights out of them. Although it sounded like my father had a good time hiding out with the waitress, the two friends refused to make any more out-of-state moonshine deliveries after that incident.

You may wonder how my father's best friend became my Pop and why I called him my step-grandfather. Those questions and many more will be answered in the following pages. You'll also learn why I'm so devoted to Pop's memory. He may not have been a really intelligent man, but he had a lot of common sense. He taught me how to survive. He taught me not to quit, not to run away from problems, and to face reality, whether it was good or bad. He taught me to look at all angles of a situation as quickly as possible before taking action. Sometimes you don't have a lot of time to do that! So, he trained me to react and think fast.

When we were hunting or fishing, he showed me the possible dangers and how to deal with them. He taught me to treat people right and with honesty and to always support my family. But he didn't take any shit off bad people. He impressed on me that if they didn't do what was right to show them the way out the door and up the road.

Pop grew up during the tough economic times of the Great Depression and formed a strong bond with my father on those shine runs. His story of "Running Shine" helped shape my impressions of what my father was like as a young man. I only wish I'd known him better.

INTRODUCTION

In my eighty-seven years of life, I've seen the good, the bad, and the ugly. But mostly the good. I've learned that while everyone may be different, we all have personal stories to tell. In many ways, our lives are a series of stories—the stories that made us who we are, the stories we hear, and the stories we tell ourselves. And if you're lucky, the good stories will outweigh the bad ones.

My Spanish ancestors arrived with the earliest explorers, and Solano, my family name, is one of the oldest in America. The origin of the name sometimes refers to "place exposed to the sun" and "an east wind." I prefer the first since I was exposed to a lot of sun growing up. But the website, *House of Names*, provides these details about the Solano name:

This place-name is derived from the word "soler," which means "site" or "plot" and it is ultimately derived from the Late Latin word "solarium," which means "bottom" or "ground."

Bottom or *ground* sounds about right since my family started at the edge, living a life of poverty, hunting, and fishing to survive. As a boy, my father cut wood and hauled it to St. Augustine by horse and buggy, where my Uncle Truman sold it as firewood. We caught mullet in homemade seine nets and sold what we didn't eat to neighbors and area stores. But along the way, Pop taught me to repair vehicles and build almost anything. Skills that served me well over the years.

Talk about living at the *bottom*: we went to the city dump at least once a month to see what valuable items we could find. We lived in a Jacksonville Beach neighborhood called Adamsville, and the city dump was only a couple of miles away through the woods. I realize it's hard for the average person to understand or even imagine that a trip to the dump was an exciting adventure for the family, but it was our version of a treasure hunt.

I remember finding old, damaged bicycles and wagons we used for parts. When we found something like that, we thought we were rich. We couldn't understand how people could throw away such good stuff.

You'll read more such stories as you page through *The Last Beach Boy*. And being of Minorcan heritage, I was born into a long line of storytellers. Pop was one of the best, and his stories formed a bridge to the past and helped shape my future. I've held these stories close to my heart and they've inspired me when times were rough and entertained me and others during the good times.

Pop's family survived by making and selling moonshine during the Prohibition Era. After rebuilding an old Model T Ford, they were able to transport and sell their product across state lines, as you read in the preface to this book.

Some of the stories you'll read are told from the perspective of a seven to ten-year-old boy being taught life lessons by his often-impatient step-grandfather Tola, or Pop as I called him. Pop had little formal education. He spoke a backcountry dialect common to that generation of Minorcans, which I, of course, accepted and absorbed. He sprinkled in a few words that you might not use in polite company, but then we were never accused of being polite company. Keep that in mind as you read about my wild childhood adventures with Pop.

Except for his Model A Ford "skeeter" motoring us over sand dunes and coquina bogs along a thirty-mile stretch of coastline from Jacksonville Beach to Vilano Beach, we were little different from those rough and tumble Minorcans of past generations following turtle crawls and casting nets for mullet. Pop had a lot of common sense and taught me lessons in life and survival I never forgot. I can still hear his voice telling me, "Bubba, life is a daily war that you are fighting to win. We win when we complete our job or whatever you're trying to do. When we build our house, we win. Build a road, we win. Go fishing and catch fish, we win. When we grow up and get married, if you marry a good person, most of the time you win."

We lived out in the country, and although Adamsville was part of Jacksonville Beach, it was mostly wilderness at the time. We hunted marsh hens, squirrels, rabbits, quail, turkey, and deer. Sometimes we ate mullet seven days a week. We sold what we didn't eat all over town to Black families and other Minorcans. The fish were plentiful, and they were cheap. We sold them for ten cents each and even more if the fish were fat during roe season.

Pop's tales swim through my mind like the mullet on the beach you'll read about. I can't swear they're one hundred percent accurate since all great storytellers, like good cake decorators, add a few additional dollops of frosting to make the story their own. You might wonder about some of the tall tales you'll read, like how we scraped barnacles off a sea turtle's nose and helped it back to the sea. Or how I drove a screwdriver through the head of a diamondback rattlesnake as big around as my leg and longer than a beach buggy. The stories remain sweet in my memory, so a little frosting doesn't hurt at all.

You'll read how I rose from a life of poverty, living off the land but learning survival skills few people ever experience. With only a high school education, I used the common sense, grit, and determination my family instilled in me to acquire multiple businesses and build a successful life for my growing family.

My fantastic journey led to financial independence and I've used my success to motivate my family and help the people I had the pleasure of working with throughout my career. As someone once said, "A rising tide lifts all boats," and I can honestly say I helped many people along the way.

There may have been some luck involved, or it may have been the rising tide of destiny that motivated and propelled me to achieve Grandma's and my dream that I promised her before she died. But I've always believed the luckiest people are those who work the hardest.

That's my story, and I'm sticking to it.

We humans have been telling stories since cavemen sat around their campfires millions of years ago, sharing experiences of hunting and killing sabertooth tigers and other wild beasts. The tales they told may have been as wild as the beasts they killed to survive, but the emotional connection these storytellers made with their fellow cavemen is the same as storytellers today. Like the cavemen and my step-grandfather Tola, I've done my share of storytelling, pulling from the reservoir of tales that are part of the incredible life journey of Bobby Solano, *The Last Beach Boy*.

CAST OF CHARACTERS

THE FIRST FAMILY

1. Albert B. Solano, Jr. —my father. Nicknames: Ally and Buck (Born December 15, 1911-Died July 14, 1942)

2. Bartola Edward Pacetti—my step-grandfather. Nicknames: Pop, Pete and Tola (Born October 20, 1911- Died October 28, 1978)

3. Margaret "Mamie" Ward Pacetti—my grandmother. Pop's wife (Born c. 1900 – Died October 1966)

4. Lorene Mary Solano—my mother. Nickname: Rene and Reenie (Born 1914 – Died 1965)

5. Joyce Solano—my sister

6. Sam Pritchard—my stepfather

7. Margie Lou Pritchard—my stepsister

8. Eugene Pritchard—my stepbrother

9. Nathan Pritchard—my stepbrother

Robert Lee Solano, Sr. (The Last Beach Boy) — Born June 5, 1935

MY FAMILY MEMBERS

1. Diane Solano—former wife and mother of all five sons

2. Robert L. Solano, Jr. —Born 1957 – Died 1969—Nickname: Bucky

3. Daniel Solano—Born 1958—wife Patty—Nickname: Dan or Danny

   a. Son David Solano married to Ashley Solano—daughter Steorra Solano

   b. Son Daniel Solano, Jr. married to Isobel Solano

   c. Daughter Sarah Solano Stokes married to Nate Stokes

   d. Son Timothy Solano — daughter Kaylyn Solano

   e. Son Joseph Solano married to Kayley Solano

4. Britt Solano—Born 1960—Nickname: Tola

    a. Son Jacob Solano

5. David R. Solano—Born 1963 – Died 2020—Nickname: Dave

    a. Daughter Kristen Solano married to Billie McKnight

        i. Roman McKnight

        ii. Bohdi McKnight

        iii. Meadow McKnight

6. Brian J. Solano—Born 1965—Nickname: Big B and Brewster

    a. Son Matthew Solano

Robert's Second Wife Karen Solano

    1. Kimberly Solano—Born 1970—Nickname: Kim and Kimz

        a. Son Rene Diaz, Jr.

    2. Bo Cannon—stepson

    3. Conner—step grandson

    4. Cory— step grandson

    5. Cody—step grandson

PART ONE

Solano Family History

Bobby's Rules to Live by:

*1. The only time you ever have in which to learn any-thing, or see anything, or feel anything, or express any feeling, or emotion, or respond to an event, or grow, or heal is this moment because this the only moment any of us ever get. You're only here now.
You're only alive in this moment.*

*2. Never have time for what you really want in life?
Then take control of the time of your life
by changing your mind.*

ONE
My Minorcan Heritage
"Everyone in town seemed to be related"

There's no way of knowing if my ancestors were among the original 1,403 colonists loaded aboard eight ships bound for the New World in 1768. Nor do we know if any Solanos or Solanas (the name sometimes ended with an *o* and sometimes with an *a*) were part of the more than 700 indentured servants who walked away from the slave-like conditions at Dr. Andrew Turnbull's New Smyrna indigo plantation. They escaped to start a new life in the nation's oldest city, St. Augustine.

The original colonists included farmers, fishermen, their wives, and children from the Mediterranean region. These included Greeks, Italians, French, and a handful of Spaniards, but most came from the island of Minorca. This is why today we're known as Minorcans.

Turnbull, an influential Scottish physician, and his partners obtained a land grant for over 100,000 acres in East Florida to start a colony to grow and supply England with a steady source of indigo. The poor colonists were eager to escape the poverty of their homelands and were promised their freedom and possibly a tract of land after serving their indenture period. But Turnbull's promises were as unreliable as the conditions they found when finally arriving in New Smyrna after a nightmarish journey during which one hundred and forty-eight people died.

After the long ocean voyage, they found the land had not been cleared, and food was scarce. To make matters worse, the ship carrying supplies for the colony had shipwrecked. Mangrove swamps had to be drained or filled before they could build shelters, and mosquitoes brought malaria. There was plenty of food in the woods, but Indians and alligators kept them close to the colony. When they could forage for food, they hunted and fished.

The poor conditions took their toll, and by 1768, four hundred and fifty people had died. But the Minorcans kept working, and the indigo plantation prospered despite the worker's brutal treatment. When their period of indenture was over, Turnbull refused to release them, and those who complained were whipped and put in stocks. After complaints reached Florida Governor Patrick Tonyn, he liberated the colonists, and during the summer of 1777, most of them walked nearly eighty miles through the wilderness to St. Augustine. There, they married into the Spanish community and into the Spanish heritage.

In his book *Finding Florida*, author T.D. Allman had this to say about the Minorcans:

Following their escape, the survivors became known collectively as "Minorcans." Settling mostly in St. Augustine, they prospered as carpenters, clerks, teachers, surveyors, shipwrights, and dentists. So did their grandchildren and their grandchildren's grandchildren. The poet Stephen Vincent Benét was one of their descendants; so was the Hollywood singing cowgirl Judy Canova. The Minorcans were the first Floridians in the modern sense. They still comprise a lively community and are the only people who can claim an unbroken Florida heritage going back further than the U.S. Declaration of Independence. Thanks to their endurance, Florida finally saw the establishment of a permanent European settlement.

And this is where we pick up the story of my Solano family—a family that survived and expanded throughout the Americas. There's a good chance my family tree predates the Minorcans, as some historians speculated that a Solana was aboard the ship carrying Pedro Menendez de Aviles to St. Augustine in

1565. That would make my family line one of the oldest in the state of Florida and North America.

"We were the first citrus growers, the first farmers, the first lumbermen, the first cattle ranchers" in Florida, said Linda Brown, co-founder of the Los Floridanos Society, which celebrates early Florida settlers, in a 2004 *Orlando Sentinel* article. On its website, losfloridanos.com, is the statement, "The settlers who arrived during the First Spanish Period, whose names included Aguilar, Diaz, Rodriguez, Sanchez, and Solana began their lives in the Presidio de San Agustin.

"In 1763, Spain ceded the Florida colony to Britain after the Seven Year War, ending the First Spanish Period. The majority of the Spanish residents, approximately 3,100, relocated to Cuba. Only a few "Los Floridanos" remained in St. Augustine to handle unsold property and settle affairs. Two of these were Manuel Solana and Francisco Sanchez. Their descendants still reside in St. Augustine."

A quick check with the MyHeritage.com website tells us that there are 877,836 records for the Solano surname and approximately 355,762 people bear the surname, many of them living in Mexico and Cuba. California has a great history of the Solano Spanish family settling there. In 1810, an Indian child named Sem-Yeto was baptized at the San Francisco Mission and named after the Spanish saint Francisco Solano. When he grew to manhood, he became a leader of his tribe and was known as Chief Solano. Solano County, part of the San Francisco Bay Area, is named after Chief Solano.

The coastal city of Solana Beach in San Diego County was originally called Lockwood Mesa. You'll often see the names Solana and Solano used interchangeably, although Solana, sometimes seen as a girl's name, means "sunshine" or "warm wind." Solano, the masculine noun, translates as "East wind" or "hot, oppressive wind."

I've found historical references to the Solano-Solana family in the Putnam County archives in Palatka, the St. Augustine Historical Society Research Library, the St. Johns County Courthouse, the P. K. Younge Library in Gaines-ville, and the Florida State Archives in Tallahassee. My earliest ancestor may have been Alonso Solana, a soldier serving his king when he arrived in St. Augustine from a village near Toledo, Spain, in the early 1600s. He remained for 75 years and established a family with deep roots throughout the country.

One historic incident involved Father Juan Joseph Solana back in the First Spanish Period, circa 1724. The St. Augustine settlement was in poor condition, and Spain provided limited aid to the colony. The soldiers stationed at Castillo de San Marcos, the fort built to defend Spain's claim to Florida, complained about the terrible conditions they had to endure. Eventually, a large group deserted and asked Father Solana for the Church's protection.

Father Solana asked the Governor for help, but instead of helping, the Governor charged the priest with harboring deserters from the Crown. He also charged Father Solana with having a wife and family in Cuba. As the conflict intensified, the Governor asked the Church in Cuba to send an emissary to investigate the charges. After holding several hearings, the emissary reported to the King about the poor conditions at the fort. Still, he became frustrated because, he said, everyone in town seemed to be related to the priest.

The story of the Minorcans is a fascinating one, and this history lesson sets the stage for the next section, where you'll learn about the strong survival streak running through my family like a "hot wind."

TWO
Family Matters
"I grew up in the middle of the woods"

The pioneers who settled in Florida were a hardy bunch. They lived off the land, hunting, and fishing, exposed to a life few of us can imagine today. I can say that was pretty much my life growing up in Adamsville during the thirties and forties. Pop taught me how to cast a net, track wild game, and make the best of every situation. I was having so much fun I seldom thought of myself as poor. But it gave me an appreciation of what life must have been like for the generations of Solanos who preceded me.

Minorcans (also called Menorcans, but I'll stick with the more popular Minorcan spelling) were a diverse group. While many made their living as fishermen, others became successful and were skilled craftsmen, plantation owners, Bishops, and army officers. But my immediate family lived a day-to-day existence, which may have affected the way I pursued success as an adult.

Like a Hollywood movie, my family story comes with twists and turns, drama, and tragedy. The only thing the Solanos had going for them was the potato farms they owned in nearby towns like Hastings and Spuds. My father was the youngest of three brothers, and his two brothers did all the farming. They weren't making much money off their potato farms during the depression and decided to sell them. One of the brothers, Uncle Truman, had left the farm to open a woodyard in St. Augustine off San Marco Boulevard on Perpall Street.

My father helped his brother by chopping wood and hauling it to Uncle

Truman's, where people would buy the wood to burn in their fireplaces and stoves. Uncle Truman sold loads of wood to Henry Flagler's fabulous Ponce de Leon Hotel, now Flagler College.

Dad was a good athlete, small, about 5'6", with black hair, brown eyes, and a dark olive complexion, displaying his Spanish roots. He might have been small, but he was strong and muscled from hard work. He played baseball for the St. Augustine city team and was so good a Jacksonville businessman recruited him to manage his company team. But I'm getting ahead of myself.

My father met Henry Kernan, a young man from New York attending St. Leo College, a Catholic institution in Central Florida. Kernan, who came from a wealthy family, relocated to St. Augustine after the Great Depression forced the college to close. His mother was dead, and his father owned a luxury hotel in Midtown Manhattan, where they lived.

My father and Kernan were about the same age, but I'm not sure how they met. They may have started as acquaintances, but that soon changed because of my Aunt Lois. My father's sister was a beauty and won the Miss St. Augustine Pageant. Kernan saw her photograph displayed in the photographer's store window, and he was captivated by her beauty. After learning Lois was my father's sister, he pleaded with Buck to introduce them.

Dad was naturally protective of his sister and wanted to shield her from this Yankee's advances, but Kernan wore him down, and after their introduction, the pair fell in love. My sister Joyce tells me they had a big wedding, moved to New York City, and lived in the hotel Henry Kernan's father owned.

ALLY & REENIE

We'll return to the hotel shortly, but first, I need to introduce you to my mother to move this story along. My father met Lorene "Reenie" Ward at a dance in Vilano Beach. Community dances were quite the thing back then, and young people would flock to them to learn the latest dance moves and find suitable partners, something young men and women have done throughout history. Reenie and my father made an instant connection and danced together the rest of the night. One of the most popular songs that year was *Body and Soul*. Perhaps the two young lovers clung to one another while a local band played the hit and swooned to the opening stanza:

> *What have you done to me*
> *I can't eat, I cannot sleep*
> *And I'm not the same anymore, no, no*
> *I don't know what to do*
> *'Cause all of me wants all of you*
> *Do I stand alone at the shore*

My father pursued Reenie and tried to court her, as they called it back then, but she was only fifteen, and my grandmother was having none of it. Dad wasn't much older at eighteen, but he wouldn't give up. Grandma had a strong will, as you'll soon learn, but eventually let them visit together after church on Sundays.

And this brings us back to Uncle Henry's Manhattan hotel. After Kernan and Lois married, he brought her to New York City, and they moved into the hotel. The move must have been exciting for the small-town girl who had never seen a big city. At some point, Uncle Henry contacted my father and told him he needed two men to help in the hotel and offered the job to Dad and his brother Wallace. Uncle Wallace was all for it, but my father didn't want to leave Reenie. He tried to persuade Grandma to let her young daughter go with him, promising to take good care of her. But Grandma wouldn't have any part of it. They went anyway and, somewhere along the way, were married. My mother, Reenie, was only sixteen at the time.

According to the story my sister Joyce heard, my Dad and Uncle Wallace became security guards for the hotel, which was across from Central Park. Aside from the hotel, Uncle Henry's father owned acres of property in Cape Canaveral, primarily a farming and fishing community at the time. In 1950, the government began constructing Port Canaveral for military and commercial purposes. The area became the test site for missiles and later launched the Mercury, Gemini, and Apollo space flights. The Kernan family sold all their property to the government but were allowed to keep their oceanfront fishing cottage.

POP PETE

As I've said, Dad and Pop were the best of friends from childhood. Neither had more than a sixth-grade education, which was common in those days, and they shared similar lifestyles. Pop's birth name was Bartola Edward Pacetti, but people called him Tola or Pete. I always called him Pop and Joyce, and later my children called him Poppa Pete or Daddy Pete.

Pop worked and lived from day-to-day, week-to-week, from mullet season to hunting season. He enjoyed living, always smiling and laughing. He drank a lot of whiskey on weekends if he had any money, either by himself or with any member of his family who would join him. During the depression, he worked for the WPA (Works Progress Administration) and helped build the road known as A1A.

You've read about how they ran moonshine for Pop's father, Camilo, in their teen years. Family lore tells us the Pacetti family was able to distill and sell illegal whiskey because Pop's oldest brother was the St. Augustine Chief of Police. Pop and my father remained close, and after Dad ran off to New York with my mother, Pop would visit Grandma to see if there was any news about his friend.

Here, I'm relying on my sister Joyce's memory, who told me that Pop would visit with Grandma after church on Sundays. My whole family was Catholic, and everybody went to church in those days. Our family didn't have a telephone back then, so face-to-face communication made the most sense. Those visits also allowed Pop a chance to get to know my grandmother better. She was quite beautiful in her day with blonde hair and blue eyes. And although she was eleven years older than Pop, they fell in love. Grandma had been divorced twice, and the Catholic Church did not allow marriages to divorced people. Doing so would mean Pop, who was deeply religious, could never receive the sacrament of Communion and was told if they married, he'd go to hell when he died.

That was enough to scare any good Catholic into toeing the line, and Grandma and Pop remained unmarried. But that would soon change, and it involved my father's baseball skills and a man credited for building the launchpads at Cape Canaveral.

Uncle Wallace was the first to become disenchanted with life in New York City and returned home. Ally and Reenie lasted for eighteen months before leaving New York behind. But while they were there, they enjoyed the big city life, and Joyce tells me their return to Florida was sparked primarily by our mother's pregnancy with her. My father, a true son of the South, didn't want his child to be born in New York City.

My sister was born in November of 1931, and the Solano family was back in St. Augustine, where my father played baseball. The sport of baseball had grown in popularity since before the turn of the last century. In those days, there were city leagues, industrial leagues, and semi-pro leagues. In 1917, a group of local businessmen started the city's professional minor league team called the St. Augustine Saints. They played in the Florida State League, won two league titles, and continued competing until 1951.

There's no record of what league Buck Solano may have played in or even what position he played. Still, his athleticism drew the interest of a Jacksonville Beach businessman named J. T. McCormick. J. T. (John Townsend) was the youngest of B.B. McCormick's four sons. B. B. (Benjamin Bachelor) was a significant force in the Beaches communities. His company, B. B. McCormick and Sons, was responsible for building much of the infrastructure in Jacksonville Beach, along with apartments, military barracks, and roads. In 1928, he won the $125,000 contract to build the future A1A from the northern St.

Johns County line south to Vilano Beach. He didn't use surveyors but constructed it by line-of-sight by staying just west of the dunes on the ocean front. Hundreds of men—including Pop—worked for a dollar a day, and McCormick had a herd of mules to haul the equipment and materials. They also dug wells at strategic points along the way to provide water for the men and mules.

J. T. later took over his father's construction company and helped expand it, but back when my father was playing baseball, J. T. was just one of the "Sons." He liked what he saw at that game and asked my father if he'd move to Jacksonville Beach to organize and manage the company's baseball team. J. T. and my father—they all knew him as Buck Solano—became good friends, and Joyce tells me the two men would go hunting together. It wasn't long before my father moved into the office as a full-time employee of B. B. McCormick and Sons.

THE MOVE TO ADAMSVILLE

My father, mother, grandmother, and young Joyce moved to Jacksonville Beach and lived in a section at the south end of the town called Adamsville, named after a Mr. Adams, who owned the property. I grew up in the middle of the woods with the Intracoastal Waterway on one side and Palm Valley just up the road.

With the help of B.B. McCormick's men and equipment, Dad and Pop constructed small wooden houses for our family and Grandma. They later added another room and an indoor bathroom. I remember helping Pop dig the hole for the septic tank at Grandma's house when I was only seven or eight years old. Before they introduced indoor plumbing, everyone used outdoor privies and showers. Grandma said the day they got indoor plumbing was the happiest day of her life.

The move to Jacksonville Beach immediately changed Pop and Grandma's relationship. Grandma's move motivated Pop to "pop" the question. Despite the Church's ruling on divorce, he proposed, and they were married. Our two houses were only about ten feet apart. The Adamsville neighborhood had few homes initially, and we had to keep the grass and weeds cut so snakes and other critters wouldn't find homes there. Eventually, more people moved in, and after Mr. Adams died, his wife sold her home to the Dorty's, who had a son my age. H. L. and I became close friends throughout our time in Jacksonville Beach together.

THREE
Losing My Father
"It left a hole in all our hearts"

My father died at the age of thirty when I was only seven years old. Losing a parent at such a young age sometimes causes serious problems as the child ages. Studies show children who lose a parent are at a higher risk for many issues, including depression, post-traumatic stress symptoms, lower self-esteem, and risk-taking behavior.

I guess I was lucky to avoid most of that, except, perhaps, the risk-taking behavior. I've always been a risk-taker and believe that was how I was raised. I thank my Pop and grandmother, along with my mother, for giving me a strong support system (my sister Joyce will tell you they spoiled me rotten) after my father died, and as you've been reading, Pop became my substitute father in every way.

I don't have a lot of memories of my father. I remember when he built a playhouse for me and my sister Joyce—and I'll share a story about one of my adventures in that playhouse in a later chapter. Sometimes my father would lose his temper and punish me for wetting the bed. Pop was the one who was always there for me, even more than my birth father. My father didn't have the patience to deal with a young boy, and his best friend, my Pop, showed me what true parental love really was.

But I must rely on my older sister about my father and his last days. She reminded me that our father had dug a pond in the backyard and lined it with concrete. Of course, ducks and geese flocked to our backyard pond, and as Joyce recalls, Dad would constantly reprimand me, telling me, "Don't swim with the ducks."

Our father suffered from asthma for most of his life. A little research will show that asthma is a chronic disease of the airways with links to the immune system. More than 26 million people in the United States have this condition. Asthma is a disease that's been traced back to the ancient Greeks. Back then, one Greek physician prescribed drinking a concoction of owl's blood and wine as a remedy.

Today we treat the condition differently—and it doesn't involve owl's blood—but when my father suffered his attacks, Dr. White would give him epinephrine injections (adrenaline). Joyce remembers when he was too sick to work at J. T. McCormick's office, and someone would bring him papers to work on at home. Here's what she recalls about Dad's death.

"My father died July 14, 1942, four months after the sinking of the oil tanker off Jacksonville Beach. I was eleven, and Bobby was seven. I remember the night we took dad to the St. Augustine hospital. I opened the car door and momma helped my father to the car. He was having a terrible asthma attack but was able to walk. He'd had asthma for most of his life and would have to take all kinds of medications, adrenaline, and stuff. Even as a little girl, I remember him taking medicines to breathe.

Momma took him to Flagler Hospital, and Dr. White kept him alive for three days before he died. He'd taken so much adrenaline to keep from choking that it got to his heart."

After Dad passed away, it left a hole in all our hearts. I was living with my mother and Joyce and ten feet away lived Grandma and Pop. Here's what happened next, according to Joyce.

When Daddy Pete went off to war, he left Grandma alone in her house. Every night we'd listen to the radio together, and Bobby would fall asleep. They doted on him and spoiled him. Pop Pete thought he was his own son, especially after daddy

died. They just clamped onto him. One day Bobby packed his bag and said he had
to move in with Grandma to protect her since Pop Pete went off to war.

And there you have the answer to why I didn't live in the same house with my mother and sister after my father died and how Pop became my substitute father. I felt my duty as the "man in the family" was to step up and protect Grandma until Pop returned from the war.

Even though our lives were in a bit of turmoil and money was scarce, Joyce reminded me that Dad's brothers had more than enough money after they sold the potato farms. Dad would have received a portion of that money, but they gave my mother only a tiny part of the proceeds because he was dead. After Pop was drafted and joined the Army Air Corps, mom worked at the USO, and Pop sent Grandma money each month from his military paycheck, but it wasn't very much.

Both my mother and Grandma were beer drinkers. They hung out at local pubs like Inkey's, where they'd spend hours socializing with friends. While they enjoyed themselves at Inkey's, I played on the beach, swam, or slept in the car. I was only seven or eight years old at the time. Pop put a stop to all that late-night drinking when he returned from the war. And with Pop back home, my "education" in the ways of nature and survival of the fittest began in earnest.

Joyce was as different from me as a cat is to a crow. She was a beautiful girl, smart as a whip, and a popular cheerleader in high school. Maybe because of her smarts and popularity, she expected more from life than the day-to-day struggles our family experienced. I understand it was tougher on a girl, especially for Joyce, who had so much going for her. But for me, I was in my element. I loved the woods and the beach and was having the time of my life.

Joyce worked throughout high school wherever she could find a job, always thinking about saving enough money to make it on her own. Then Lady Luck came her way. She said her prayers were answered when she met Hank Boyer. Hank said she was the answer to his prayers too, and they became high school sweethearts. They married after Hank went to Stetson College on a football scholarship.

Hank had a distinguished army career, serving in Vietnam, later teaching military history at Loyola College in Maryland, and becoming a Lt. Colonel. Later, the army sent him and Joyce to France on what my sister said was some "secret spy business."

I'm proud of my big sister, but while she was making her way in life, I was with Pop, confronting boars and rattlers in the scrublands, turtle poachers on the beach, and had my own frightening experience with a Florida panther. Despite the danger, I saw it all as an opportunity and exposure to a life very few people ever encounter. I was out there challenging the world with Pop as my guide, roaming the woods, riding our skeeter over sand dunes, constantly fishing, and hunting. What boy wouldn't love it? Did I miss my father? Sure, but I was lucky enough to have another set of loving "parents" living next door.

Part Two of *The Last Beach Boy* focuses on my many youthful adventures and how they helped shape my future life. But first, you need to hear about my grandmother's early years. Hers is a remarkable story that might remind you of a work of fiction filled with conflict, danger, and heartbreak, but it's all true and illustrates Grandma's toughness. So, read on.

Bobby's father, Albert "Ally" Solano, Jr., who died at the age of thirty, when Bobby was only seven.

Bartola "Pete" Pacetti, Pop to Bobby, played an important role in his life.

Albert Solano with his two young children, Joyce and Bobby.

FOUR
Grandma's Story
"She believed she had divine help"

My grandmother Mamie was an unbelievable woman, tough as nails and not one to back down when she knew she was right. Born in 1900 into a family of strawberry farmers in Plant City, Florida, she had three sisters and one brother. Her mother died when she was only six years old, and her father struggled to care for all the children and run his farm. He eventually made the difficult decision to part with some of the children.

My sister Joyce remembers Grandma's story somewhat differently than I do. Joyce told me that a country doctor named Davis cared for Grandma's family and their animals, so possibly he was a veterinarian. Dr. Davis was a widower with children of his own, and he saw the opportunity to help solve both of their problems by taking young Mamie. Adopting her, you might think, but no. He had other plans in mind. Perhaps Dr. Davis bartered his services or paid cash in exchange for young Mamie, but she was only thirteen years old when he married her. That's the way they did things back then.

My Grandma said she was treated like a slave, cooking, cleaning, taking care of the house, and tending to his three kids. Sometimes her husband's kin folks would come around for supper, and she had to fix dinner for them as well. Grandma wasn't one to suffer in silence. When she complained or threatened to run away, Dr. Davis tried to intimidate her, according to my sister, threatening her by saying he came from a wealthy and powerful family that could harm her and her family.

One year after they married, Grandma gave birth to my mother, Mary Lo-rene. The year was 1914, and Grandma was only fourteen years old. Imagine the state of mind of a fourteen-year-old with a baby. She not only had to care for her child but also for Dr. Davis and his three children. The situation must have been intolerable.

Grandma told me she became friends with an older girl who lived nearby. This girl's life was even more horrible than Grandma's, and she was looking for a way out. The girl told Mamie how her father beat her when he drank. Grandma said he did other things to her, but she kept those details to herself, leaving them to my imagination.

My mother was two years old when Grandma and her friend decided they'd had enough and began plotting an escape. The two girls slipped out of their houses after everyone was asleep and would huddle together and talk about the terrible things they were enduring and how their lives might be different if they could only escape.

After Grandma's girlfriend turned eighteen, she told Mamie she had a job working on a cruise ship out of Miami. "I'm going to take it, and I want you to come with me," she said.

She told Grandma she could get her a job as a maid on the ship. "But you have to sign up for two years." She had also stolen enough money from her father over the last three years to pay for their bus fare to Miami.

Grandma made up her mind to follow her friend to Miami and take the job on the ship. But she couldn't take her baby, my mother, with her. Grandma had become close to Dr. Davis's oldest daughter Trish. After pledging Trish to silence about her plans to leave, Grandma asked her to care for little Lorene until she returned. The girl agreed, but Grandma said it almost killed her to think about leaving her baby. But she saw this as her only chance to get herself and Lorene out of that miserable place once and for all.

She couldn't stop hugging and kissing Lorene when the big day arrived.

My mother cried and carried on like she knew her mother was about to leave. Grandma lingered at the baby's crib until sometime after midnight, waiting for her daughter to fall asleep. Eventually, she crept away to meet her friend at Dr. Davis's mailbox, about a half-mile from the house. Grandma had told her friend to go on without her if she hadn't arrived by 2 a.m. Luckily, she made it on time, although she admitted she almost backed out.

As they trudged down the dark road, Grandma couldn't stop crying. She said she cried for two days. Every time she thought about her baby, she'd burst into tears. The two young women had to walk over five miles to the highway, carrying with them what little belongings they owned. Once they reached the highway, they hitched a ride to Lake City and, from there, caught the bus to Jacksonville, where they transferred to a Miami-bound bus.

Grandma talked little about her job on the cruise ship, but she did tell me she was one of the ladies who cleaned the cabins and did the laundry. She shared a room on the bottom deck of the ship where they housed most of the staff. They got very little time off, although occasionally, when they were in port, they would go ashore for their day off. Joyce recalls Grandma telling her the ship traveled to Cuba and back and may have made an occasional stop in St. Augustine.

When they had an extended layover in Miami, she immediately caught a bus home to see baby Lorene. She said she cried the entire way to Lake City. People tried to comfort her, but she was too emotional to stop crying. She paid for a cab in Lake City instead of hitching a ride to the farm. Arriving at the doctor's home, she noticed a mud-stained little girl with matted hair playing in the dirt. She had to look twice before she recognized her daughter. Grandma told me that seeing Lorene in such a state, covered with scratches and boils, was like a punch to the stomach. It made her feel even more guilty for leaving her behind.

She picked up her child and hugged her so tightly she thought she might hurt her. Dr. Davis wasn't home, but his youngest daughter emerged from the house, yelling at Grandma, "You put that baby down right now." The girl didn't recognize Grandma at first, and when Grandma asked where her older sister Trish was, she said Trish had run away with one of the field hands about a year ago. No one had heard from her since.

Grandma took my mother inside, bathed her, and doctored her sores. Then she dressed her in clean clothes. When her husband came home, he began screaming at her to leave. He said he'd kill her before letting her take Mary Lorene. After much pleading, Grandma finally talked him into letting her stay for a couple of days by agreeing to clean the house and cook. He grudgingly agreed but insisted she'd have to sleep with him too.

She knew what she had to do, and on the second day, she waited until her husband was asleep and quietly slipped out of the bedroom. She found the bag she'd already packed and carefully picked up Mary Lorene so as not to awaken her. Together, mother and child slipped out of the house into the darkness.

She was mistaken if she thought she'd made her escape and put all the meanness behind her. Before long, she heard her husband's dogs howling and barking. He must have awakened, found his wife and daughter missing, and turned the dogs loose on her. His dogs were trained to trail by scent for deer, hogs, coons, and people. They were mixed breeds of bloodhounds and redbone hounds, descendants of the hounds that used to hunt run-away slaves for plantation owners.

Grandma knew she had to throw them off her trail, but how? Then she thought of the creek on the other side of the corn field adjoining the road where she was walking. She took off through the corn field, telling me it was hard going at night, and she tripped and fell many times. Tough corn stalks and stems pulled at her clothes and scratched her arms, but she kept going. Her determination to get away with her child was stronger than all the corn fields in the south.

She waded into the creek, clutching my mother in her arms, and sloshed through the shallow water. The water rose higher as she moved further south, climbing above her knees until it was waist deep. She heard the dogs barking in the distance, but it sounded like they were getting closer. Soon the creek widened, and she stumbled on a small island about twenty feet from the bank. She crawled onto the spit of land and curled into a ball with her baby in her arms. Her clothes were soaked, and she shivered in the chill night air. She wrapped her arms around Lorene, doing her best to keep her warm. She prayed her child would stay quiet and not cry out and alert the howling dogs.

When the hounds abruptly stopped barking, she figured they'd tracked her scent to the creek and were trying to find it again. She said she had never prayed so hard in her life. Grandma heard the dogs scuffling around, and the sounds of horses and voices carried in the still night air. She thought she recognized her husband's voice and some of his field hands as they talked in hushed tones. And they were getting closer.

Then everything went quiet.

Grandma waited until she was sure they were gone and began moving again. She understood she needed to be far away before the sun came up. Looking back on that night, my grandmother told me she didn't know how she made it out of the creek to the other side, across another field to a graded farm road. All of it in the dark while carrying my mother and the bag she toted with them. She believed she had divine help.

She stopped and rested when she reached the road on the other side of the field. Divine intervention stepped in again when a truck carrying a load of watermelons came along just as the sun was rising. The truck driver braked when he saw my poor grandmother holding a baby and waving for him to stop. He gave her a ride to the Lake City Produce Market, and from there, she walked to the bus station. She took the bus to St. Augustine, where her brother, Uncle Raymond, was living at the time. Grandma started her new life in St. Augustine with my mother and the help of her brother. But it wasn't easy because, for over a year, her husband sent people to St. Augustine to look for Grandma and her baby.

Hearing this story makes it easier to understand why Grandma was so protective of her fifteen-year-old daughter when Ally Solano came courting. Of course, I'm glad the two young lovers ran off together and became man and wife, or I wouldn't be around to share this story.

When Grandma told me of her incredible escape, I thought about how precious life is and how miracles really happen.

PART TWO

The Beach Life

Bobby's Rules to Live by:

3. All that truly matters in the end is that you loved during this life family and friends, more than once.

4. What other people think of you is none of your business.

5. Don't take yourself so seriously. No one else does.

ONE

Growing Up on the Beach
"The beach made me a different kind of person"

Things have changed since the days we rode up and down the beach. That's not allowed today, but if you could, you'd pass dozens of multi-million-dollar homes and condominiums. Sure, there's a sprinkling of older homes at the north and south ends, but in between, particularly in upscale Ponte Vedra Beach, you'd be hard pressed to find a home selling for less than $2 million.

Things were different growing up, riding in my Pop's skeeter, searching for turtle crawls or schools of mullet. Back then, we'd drive for hours without seeing more than a few houses. We passed high-rise sand dunes but no high-rise condominiums. I read somewhere that in 1960, you could buy an oceanfront lot in Ponte Vedra Beach for $30,000. Today, you could probably count the available oceanfront properties on the fingers of one hand, and they would cost at least a million dollars.

There were no houses on the ocean after you left Mickler's Pier heading south when I was growing up. I remember riding along the beach with Pop one day and seeing nothing but ocean and miles and miles of dunes. "Who owns all these sand dunes along the beach?" I asked Pop.

"I don't know," he said. "Must be the government but what good are they? There's nothing but rattlesnakes and thick bushes between the dunes and the hard road."

He was referring to A1A, the scenic highway that runs along the Atlantic

Ocean from Key West to Fernandina Beach. He was familiar with the northern stretch of road because he helped build it.

"Nobody will ever do anything with them," he continued. "That's just some extra land the Good Lord thought of for the animals—the snakes, and the birds."

I spent most of my childhood and teen years on the beach. The early years were part of my education as Pop taught me about nature and how to live off Mother Nature's bounty. I don't want you to get the idea that the Solanos had a home on the beach like some of my high school classmates. Adamsville, where we lived, was low-rent property and about two miles from the coast. We drove down 16th Avenue onto the beach more times than I can remember, so I consider myself a Beach Boy and believe the beach made me a different person.

What do I mean by that? The smell of the ocean and the summer breezes on your skin were second nature to us. Watching the waves roll in is both peaceful and awe-inspiring. My experiences on the beach with Pop and later with my friends helped shape my values and how I view the world. I think that being on the beach is the best therapy session ever.

The beach life probably made me more relaxed and positive, and it helped me understand the importance of family since we spent so much time on the shore and in the water. I experienced a lifetime of adventures on the beach and invite you to take an imaginary seat next to eight-year-old Bobby Solano in Pop's skeeter as I relive some of my beach memories.

TWO

Mr. Billy Goat

"He took off like a shot"

I was a young boy when my father brought home a Billy goat. This was one of my last memories of my dad since he died soon after. Billy was two years old and already set in his ways. As he aged, he grew a long beard and liked to cock his leg up to pee, soaking his beard and staining it yellow.

You had to keep an eye on the old goat because he had a mean streak, and if you turned your back on him, Mr. Billy would introduce his head to your backside. Headbutting is normal for goats when they're playing with other goats, but you don't want to be attacked by your pet whenever you get near him. My Grandma had several painful encounters with Billy Goat Gruff when she tried to feed him and developed an intense dislike of the beast.

A few years later, Pop made me a little two-wheel cart with a harness for Billy. Can you see where this is going? Pop hooked Billy up to the cart, and we practiced riding around the yard. I had reins to guide him and a switch to get his attention. Pop walked alongside me as I practiced driving the Billy cart. Then I was ready for my solo ride, believing I would be guiding Billy, but soon learned he was the one in control. I harnessed Billy up, climbed aboard the cart, popped the reins, and told him to Giddy up. I could have been talking to a wall because the stubborn goat wouldn't budge. I tried again, urging him to move in a louder voice. Nothing. I tried pleading, "C'mon, Billy, pretty please."

Old Billy was having none of it, and I ended up pulling Billy down the road with him bucking and pulling against me every step of the way. I finally gave up and turned him around toward the house. Now the goat decided it was time to move. As I scrambled to jump back into the cart, he took off like a shot. Billy flew down the road while I hung on for dear life. The gate to his pen was open, but first, he trampled through Grandma's rose garden, knocked over her potted plants, and then blasted toward his pen.

My heart was beating like a jackhammer, but I thought he would stop and walk into the pen. Instead, he hit the fence at full speed and knocked both wheels off the cart before rushing into his little house. That marked the conclusion of my goat carting career, but not the end of the goat drama.

Grandma was so upset with Billy that she had Pop chain him inside the pen so he wouldn't butt her during feeding time. That might have been enough to restrain some critters, but old Billy had other plans. The first time Grandma ventured into the pen to feed the old goat, Billy dashed out and managed to wrap the chain around her legs, pulling her to the ground. Not content with knocking her down, Billy began butting her as she lay there screaming for help. Pop rushed to the rescue, untangled her from the chains, and got her safely out of the pen.

That was the final straw for Grandma. I don't think I'd ever seen her so mad. She told Pop, "I'm going to kill that son of a bitch as soon as you're not around."

And she meant it. Pop got the message. He told me, "Bubba, Billy's got to go, or your grandma will kill him.

And one of my first adventures came to an end. Goodbye, Mr. Billy Goat.

THREE
Big Ditch Disaster
"I was having a hard time breathing"

As you know, I grew up in a small community called Adamsville, at the extreme south end of Jacksonville Beach on the Duval and St. Johns County line. To the south of us was Ponte Vedra Beach, which at one time had more mules and wild cows than people. Back then, they called it Mineral City because the National Lead Company was mining valuable minerals from a thirteen-mile stretch of beachfront it owned. After World War I, there was little demand for the minerals, and the company decided to develop the area into a resort community like The Cloister in Sea Island, Georgia. The development manager found the name Pontevedra on a map of Spain, and soon after, Mineral City became Ponte Vedra Beach.

Palm Valley was a rural community on the west side of highway A1A located on the inland waterway, running from the mouth of the St. Johns River on the north down to St. Augustine and the Matanzas Inlet on the south. We called the canal the "Big Ditch." A little internet research tells us that Palm Valley was once known as Diego Plains after Don Diego Espinoza, a Spanish nobleman who had settled in the area known today as Palm Valley. In 1908, a canal was dug through Diego Plains, connecting the San Pablo River with the Tolomato River near St. Augustine to the south. This Intracoastal canal made access to the valley much easier for the residents that had settled in this area.

Technically this isn't a beach story, but close enough in my mind. Palm

Valley was only a two-mile walk through the woods from our house, and as a young boy, my friends and I would walk along the Big Ditch, playing in and around the waterway. When they dug the canal, they left huge mounds of dirt on both sides of the waterway. Being kids, we'd dig tunnels and underground clubhouses in the dirt piles. Black folks lived close by, in a neighborhood on the other of the canal. They mostly stayed on their side of the Intracoastal, but two Black kids—Tim and his younger brother Joseph—often joined us. We didn't have a problem playing with the Black kids and always invited them over to play with us. But Tim and Joseph were the only two who showed up. Maybe the others felt funny playing with white kids.

One day Tim, who was my age, twelve, Joseph, and me were digging a tunnel in the mountain of earth next to the Big Ditch. I was digging while Tim shoveled the dirt back and out of the entrance to our tunnel. Suddenly the roof above Tim caved in on him without warning.

Everything went black. I couldn't see my hand in front of my face. Tim was yelling and crying, and I crawled over to him and tried to calm him down. "It's okay, Tim, we're alive. Joseph is outside, and I'm sure he'll get help." I didn't know that for a fact but hoped it was true.

The dirt had covered Tim up to his stomach, and he was still wailing. "Let's get you out of that dirt," I said, pulling the dirt away from him as fast as I could. But the more soil I moved, the more that fell on us. After a few minutes, the dirt stopped falling, and I dug Tim out, but we remained trapped in our underground tunnel.

I was covered with dirt and sweating like a hog. It was hot and stuffy, and I was having a hard time breathing. Then it struck me: Oxygen! We must have been running low on air. I didn't say anything to Tim since he was upset, but I told him to start digging. We began pulling the dirt back away from the cave-in toward the entrance.

"Keep digging," I told Tim. "I'm sure Joseph must be digging from the outside and in a few minutes, we'll see daylight."

I may have sounded brave for Tim's sake, but inside I was just as scared as he was. I knew we were only three or four feet from the entrance, and it shouldn't take long to break through to the outside, but I worried about how much more dirt would fall on us as we dug. Tim's brother Joseph was only eight years old, but I hoped he had enough sense to either go for help or keep digging.

The heat inside that tunnel was stifling. I felt if we didn't get out soon, I'd suffocate. But I kept digging, and just as Tim began crying again, a sliver of light broke the darkness. We heard Joseph calling for us.

"Are ya'all all right," he yelled.

I said, "No, we're both dead, but get us out anyway."

Now we could hear other people talking and the scrape of shovels digging. Before long, there was a hole big enough for us to crawl out. I pulled at Tim and told him to go first. Then I crawled out after him. Man, was I glad to see daylight again. We saw that a bunch of people had come over to help and were thankful.

I can tell you that was the end of our cave-building adventures in the Big Ditch.

FOUR
Turtle Crawls and Turtle Poachers
"What is a two-legged varmint?"

At about nine on a Saturday night, Pop and I motored down to the beach using the 36th Avenue ramp at Jacksonville Beach. We were at war, and Pop was home on leave from the Army Air Corps. Pop was driving his Model A Ford skeeter. We hit the sand and headed south to our usual destinations, Ponte Vedra Beach and St. Augustine. The night was black, and without the headlights, we would have wandered into the water, but Pop said we'd see a full moon coming up over the ocean around ten.

As we approached the St. Johns County boundary, we slowed to squeeze through the poles set across the beach from the tide line up to the dunes. Whoever had planted those poles made a couple of mistakes in their measurements, and there was one gap just large enough for us to drive through. After we first discovered the error, we marked an X on the poles, so we could see them quickly without stopping.

Every time we made this drive, Pop would complain and cuss about the "damn rich folks" trying to keep hard-working fishermen out. "Folks are getting mad as hell about these poles," he said, adding a few choice expletives.

A few years later, when Pop was still cursing the rich folks, I spoke up and said, "I'm afraid it's only going to get worse. More people are building houses along the beach, and there's a lot of money in Ponte Vedra that will force them to block it off even more. I heard they'll start fining people that go through these poles if they catch them."

Pop didn't agree. He said, "Bubba, I think they're not going to be able to stop the fishermen from catching fish on the beach. A lot of these mullet fishermen make their living that way. Those Minorcan fishermen will start shooting people if they block them from catching fish on the beach and hunting turtle eggs. The beach was made by God for all the people not just the rich ones and the law. So, they'll be a lot of fighting going on before it's over."

On that earlier outing, we continued our ride until we approached the second set of poles at the south end of Ponte Vedra Beach, right in front of the Ponte Vedra Inn clubhouse. The clubhouse was about a mile from the Oasis Bar and Liquor Store, or Barney's as everyone called it since Barney Compton owned it.

Pop squeezed our skeeter past the poles high up on the side of the dunes. The people that buried those poles forgot about dune buggies like ours with big balloon tires. We could go anywhere over the soft sand and the dunes.

After getting around the poles, Pop pulled up to Barney's drive-through window and asked Barney for a pint of Old Crow. Mr. Barney was Pop's friend, and Pop always brought him some mullet on his way home if he had caught any. Mr. Barney said, "Tola, bring me some mullet when you come back, and I'll give you half a pint of whiskey for free next trip."

Pop agreed and told him he'd leave the fish in the cooler in his generator shed.

Barney said, "Thanks Tola. You're a good nigger."

Barney's had a ramp going down to the beach that was nothing more than soft sand, which Mr. Barney would smooth out now and then. But cars quickly cut ruts into the sand, and on Saturdays and Sundays, a lot of them would get stuck there.

"Pop, why don't Mr. Barney fix this runway so people can get down to the beach without getting stuck?"

Pop said, "You saw that big old wrecker Barney's got, didn't you?"

Everybody had seen Barney's wrecker, and Pop explained, "Well, Barney makes money pulling cars out that get stuck in the runway. When summer comes and there's a lot of cars on the beach and the tide starts coming in it traps some of these Georgia crackers' cars and Barney pulls them out and charges them a wrecker fee. So, I don't think he wants the damn ramp fixed. He pulls out cars from all over this end of the beach all the way to Mickler's Pier and sometimes beyond. But if Barney has to go far down the beach, it's going to cost them an arm and a leg. You can bet on that."

I knew Mr. Barney sometimes asked Pop to drive the wrecker for him in the summer when he was busy and couldn't leave his bar, sharing the towing fee with him.

Mr. Barney had two pretty daughters. One was about my age, and her name was Martha Compton. I forget the other sister's name but remember she was cute. When I was older, I'd sometimes daydream about taking them for a beach ride in my skeeter.

Pop was home on leave after his basic training when we took this beach ride looking for turtle crawls and mullet to net. After he joined the Army Air Corps, they sent him to Italy because he was Italian. They needed his masonry experience to build airstrips, houses, aircraft hangars, and bunkers. I don't remember how many days he was home on leave, but he loved the beach and throwing his net. And boy did I love it too.

You never knew what you were going to run into on the beach. It was wide-open, nothing but sand, dunes, and coquina shells. Part of the beach south of Mickler's Pier was an area we called the Graveyard because it had claimed a lot of cars over the years. Cars and trucks became stuck in the soft, wet coquina shells, and they could say goodbye to their vehicles when the tide came in.

Pop might have been small in stature, but he had big arms and a big chest from years of hard work picking up bricks and stones and plastering the outside and inside of buildings. His people had always done plaster and masonry work. I guess the skill was passed down through the generations. That's what he was raised and taught to do. You do it because you gotta do it.

The moon peaked above the ocean as we drove south past Barney's. It shone over the water, reflecting a shimmering ribbon from the horizon to the shore. Pop said we were going to see some turtle crawls tonight.

"How do you know that?" I asked him.

"Cause turtles crawl on full moons, and the tide comes high. The full moon helps the turtle to see how to get back to the water. The turtles lay around in the water, sometimes for a day or two, waiting for the full moon."

"How you know all that about them turtles, Pop?"

Pop must have taken my question wrong because he snapped, "Now you listen to me, Bubba. First of all, because I said so. Don't be questioning your elders, or I'll knock a knot on your head. Understand me?"

"Pop I didn't mean to question you. I was just wondering how you learned all that." I loved Pop, but maybe he expected too much from an eight-year-old boy.

He said, "Well stop your wondering so much and asking so many fool questions. I learned most of them from actually being with my dad when I was growing up. Sometimes he would tell me what he wanted me to know, but most of the time I watched and listened. So, you watch and listen more."

"Yes sir, I will." And I did.

The tide was about halfway up the beach, and we were riding along on what they call the dune tides, which is where the normal high tide stopped. The lower dunes were flat soft sand that led up to the higher dunes covered with sea oats.

Pop decided to test me and said, "What does it mean if you are riding along on the beach at night and you see a single turtle crawl going up the beach towards the high dunes? You know turtles only crawl at night to lay their eggs."

I had to ask, "Why do they only crawl at night Pop?"

"Because they trying to stay away from danger. They don't want animals and people to know where they lay their eggs. Sometimes the old turtle will make three or four wallows in the sand to confuse animals or humans from finding where she buried her eggs. Now I asked you about the one crawl. What does that mean about the turtle?"

I said I didn't know, and he said, "Well, think about it. Use your head for something besides a hat rack. What the hell does one crawl mean?"

Pop had a lot of natural knowledge in his head, but one thing he lacked was patience. He spat out, "Damn it! It means the turtle is up on the high watermark looking for a place to lay her eggs. She might have already started laying them, you got me?"

I got him. But one thing I didn't get at first was the turtle crawl. I thought it meant the turtle was crawling, but the crawl referred to the track the sea turtle made heaving her heavy body from the water to the high soft sand where she would dig her body pit or nest to lay her eggs.

"Now the first thing you do when you see that one track going up the beach towards the dunes is turn your headlights off right away." Pop was continuing the lesson to his young apprentice. "You get out of your Skeeter and follow the single set of tracks up toward the sand dunes. Keep your flashlight down real low and never flash it on the turtle. Before you going to ask me why, dammit, I'll tell you. Any light flashed on her confuses her and she doesn't know which way to go. Also she thinks the light could be some kind of a danger. She might think it's the moon shining and get all confused which way is back to the ocean. So don't let anybody ever shine light in her eyes. Got me?"

"Yes sir, I understand."

"Now if you see two crawls in your head lights, you know the turtle has come up, laid her eggs, and gone back to the water. There is a lot of other stuff I can tell you about the turtles, but it would take all night. But I will tell you I have seen a turtle come up on the beach where a seawall has been put down. She crawled along the seawall but could not find any sand that was above the high tide waves. She gave up and went back to the water, guess she was going to come up someplace else after she rested. Somehow, they know when they are out of reach of the high-water mark before they go to lay their eggs. All right let's get back to watching the beach, we could come up on a crawl before you know it, or even on the turtle going up or coming down, so you need to keep your eyes peeled."

Pop carried a sawed-off double barrel shotgun between the two bucket seats in our Model A Ford. He kept the shotgun loaded with double ought buckshot. The gun had two hammers that you pulled back and locked. When you pulled the trigger, they hit the firing pins, and that thing could blow one hell of a hole in something. Pop named his gun Old Betsy. I asked him one day why he carried the shotgun in the skeeter. He said it was for four-legged and two-legged varmints.

"Pop, I know what four-legged varmints look like but what is a two-legged varmint?"

"Damn boy, you sure are stupid sometimes. Two legged varmints are bad people. You understand what I mean by bad people?"

Yes, sir was my standard answer whenever Pop asked me if I got it or understood, and I said it once again. This night, Pop was more interested in finding a turtle crawl than catching mullet as we drove toward St. Augustine but said we'd fish on the way back.

With the full moon, he thought we should be able to spot a crawl and possibly find a loggerhead digging her nest. Once the turtle decides where to make her nest, she starts digging the hole with her back flippers and makes a perfect hole—large at the bottom and smaller at the top like a vase. Her flipper goes down in the hole, swirls around, and she uses it to scoop out the sand. Just like we'd scoop a handful of sand, she lifts it and throws it out of the way. If you're there watching and not careful, you will get a face full of sand. I tell you this from first-hand experience. When she finishes digging the egg chamber, she lays between 80 and 120 eggs the size of ping-pong balls and then covers them with the sand using her rear flippers.

Pop told me there was an unwritten law amongst the fisherman and hunters not to harm the turtles or remove more than half the eggs, which we never did. We took the eggs to eat and to sell, especially to other Minorcans who loved to boil them, which by the way, do not get hard when you boil them. We'd pinch open the eggshell, put Datil pepper sauce in the hole, and squeeze the soft shell until the inside slides out into your mouth.

Pop liked to say that eating turtle eggs makes your dick get harder. At eight years old, I wasn't sure why you'd want your dick to get harder, but I knew better than to question him because he would've called me stupid. So, I let that one go.

The tide was still coming in. Pop was driving between the rising tidal pools and the high tide dune. The skeeter would sometimes slide in the coquina towards the tidal pool, and Pop would have to pull the skeeter up higher on the dune. But this was just an ordinary situation for Pop, who had been driving on the beach all his life. He was always up for a challenge, and I was soaking it all in, sitting in the bucket seat beside him.

Before long, we arrived at Mickler's Pier, where a paved path came down through the dunes from A1A. There were pilings in the water left over from an old pier, and you had to be careful not to run into them when you were running down the beach at night because they popped up quick in your head-lights.

We saw a few people at the pier drinking beer around driftwood fires hav-ing a good time. Pop rolled on by, and soon we entered the Graveyard. The Graveyard got its name because the coquina was deep and wet, and your skee-ter, jeep, or car could quickly sink up to the axles. If you weren't a good driver, you were stuck. Your only way out at that point was to call Mr. Barney or get someone to pull you out. But Pop knew what to do if we ran into a soft co-quina bed. He'd shift into second gear and quickly steer out towards the dune.

Most people didn't know how to maneuver in the Graveyard, and many people lost their cars when the tide came in before they could get Mr. Barney or someone to pull them out.

We were almost through the Graveyard when suddenly the front tires went down in a wet coquina bed, bringing us to a sudden standstill like we'd hit a wall. I was thrown against the dashboard, busted my lip, and bloodied my nose. Pop said hold on. He threw it in reverse as fast as he could, spinning the wheels but moving backward. Pop backed us out of the bed as quickly as he could before we sank deeper into the wet coquina bed. He was racing back-wards and started turning the steering wheel toward the high-water mark. You could feel the tires biting into solid ground as we moved away from the water and toward the dunes. Then he stopped and said, "Well boy, we shore nuff just got out of that one by a hair. And I mean a cunt hair."

I didn't know the difference between the two hairs but nodded in agree-ment.

He asked me to hand him the liquor bottle he'd bought at Barney's and took a long swallow. He looked at me and asked, "That nose of yours stop bleeding yet?"

I said I was okay. That was a lie because it hurt like hell. He said, "I told you to hold on all the time when you riding this beach. You never know when something like that going to happen. Didn't I tell you that?"

I nodded and repeated another, "Yes sir."

"Then damn it, hold on, you hear me?"

"Yes sir, I hear you."

We got past the Graveyard without any more problems and were approaching the first well. The artesian water well was set in a circular concrete pool about two to three feet deep. The red brick wells were drilled during the depression when Mr. McCormick won a contract from the WPA to extend the highway from Jacksonville Beach to St. Augustine. But before reaching the well, Pop slowed and said, "Hey, I see something up ahead."

Sure enough, it was a Model A Ford truck with a wooden stake body and no lights on. Pop eased closer to the truck, and we saw three men, two whites and one Black, standing around a big loggerhead turtle flipped over on her back. She was still alive, and her big flippers were flopping helplessly in the air. The men carried ugly curved knives, and it was apparent what they intended to do to that turtle.

Pop flipped on the high beams and coasted the skeeter to within ten yards of the men before stopping. "Bubba, you sit right here in the skeeter." He reached down between the seats and pulled out Old Betsy. He said, "Remember the two-legged varmints you asked about? Well, here they are."

He climbed out of the old Ford and stepped up next to the headlights where he could see the men and the turtle, but they had a hard time seeing him. He held Old Betsy out so the men with the knives could see the outline of his shotgun

The older of the three men yelled at Pop, "Hey back off, and cut those damn lights off. They're blinding us. What the hell do you want anyway?"

Pop said, "What I want is for you three guys to flip that turtle back over on its belly and the three of you help her back to the water."

One of the other men screamed, "You go to hell! This is our turtle, and we aim to butcher it right here old man."

Pop slowly raised Old Betsy and aimed the double barrel shotgun at the picket wood bed of the truck. He cocked one hammer and pulled the trigger. With an ear-splitting blast, the buckshot tore through the wooden stakes, shooting splinters everywhere. It took a minute for the smoke to clear.

Again, one of the guys popped off. "You crazy son of a bitch. You lost your mind?"

The older man spoke up quickly and said, "Shut up Buster. This stupid bastard will blow us to Kingdom Come with that goddamn shotgun." He turned to Pop and said, "Okay, old man, what you want?"

Pop said, "I told you I want you three guys to flip that turtle over and help her get back into the water. Now that's very simple."

The older man, who I assumed was the boss, told the other two men to put their knives in the truck. Then they gathered around the heavy loggerhead, which can weigh up to 350 pounds, and flipped her over. The turtle was exhausted and tried to move but didn't get far. She was moving in the wrong direction. Pop ordered them to turn her around and help her to the water. They glared at him for a moment but slowly got her turned around.

Pop stood in the same spot the whole time, cradling Old Betsy without moving. We watched the turtle as she hit the first wave and then started stroking into the deep water before disappearing.

The three men walked to their truck, their eyes shooting daggers at Pop as they moved. Before getting in the buckshot-damaged truck, the older man said to Pop, "We'll meet again and maybe the odds will be different."

Pop pointed Old Betsy at him and said, "You better hope we don't meet again."

The truck jerked out in front of us and headed south toward St Augustine. Pop watched them drive away until the taillights flickered out in the distance to be sure it wasn't stopping. He walked back to the driver's side, breached Old Betsy, and took the empty shell out. He reloaded the weapon before replacing her between the seats.

"I think we better head back towards the house to see if we can catch a mullet on the way back. It's not a good idea to run into those three hombres again tonight. Don't think it would be healthy for none of us. Keep an eye out now for a turtle crawl, they crawl a lot around Mickler's Pier sometimes."

Sure, enough, in a few miles we spotted a crawl. There was only a single track, so I said, "That means she's up there laying, right Pop?"

He agreed, eased the skeeter to a stop, and cut off the lights and engine. One thing Pop taught me about stopping on the beach is never to brake hard. When you brake hard on the beach, the tires dig into the sand, sometimes breaking the hard top layer, and Bam! You find yourself in a hole and stuck.

Pop got his flashlight, and we quietly headed over the high-water dunes to find the turtle's nest. Pop said, "If she is digging the hole where she'll lay her eggs or still looking for her nest area, you cannot make any noise or shine any lights around her. That will make her stop and head back to the water because she senses danger for her eggs. If she has finished digging her egg hole and if she has started laying eggs, she is not going to stop laying. Keep your voice low if you have anything to say."

Pop told me the turtle digs her egg hole with her two back flippers, and it is usually perfect unless she has a damaged rear flipper. "I saw one with half the flipper missing. Probably bit off by a shark when she was younger," he once told me.

At the turtle's nest, we watched the big loggerhead's body contracting as she continued laying her eggs. Pop reached into the hole and pulled out some eggs. He'd told me that we never take more than half of them. We leave half to hatch to keep nature going. He put the eggs in a bag he had tied to his belt, and we continued to watch the turtle.

Pop pointed down at her, "She got herself a heavy load of barnacles. Go to the skeeter and bring me the big tire tool." I took off, retrieved the tool, and headed back, trying not to make any noise.

"Now watch," he whispered to me." Using the flat end of the lug wrench, he gently tapped the barnacles from her shell. Tapping with his hand, they popped right off. He went over the turtle's entire back and even removed some on top of her head. Pop said, "There you are, girl. Got some of that weight off you."

I asked him if the barnacles would kill her. He said they usually just slow her down and are a drag against her swimming unless they get way out of control as she gets older. She has to be able to move quickly to get away from her enemies like sharks and rays. Also, shrimp nets kill a lot of turtles.

"But those men we saw tonight kill the most adult turtles to sell their meat to restaurants and meat plants. Someday there will be a law against catching the turtles on the beach, and killing them when they trying to lay their eggs."

And he was right. In 1967 they passed the endangered species law that stopped most of the killing on the beach and they even included a rule that the shrimp boats had to fix their nets to let out any turtles caught in them.

Pop wanted to wait for the turtle to finish packing her nest and be sure she got back in the water without any problems. We sat there, and he told me some other things about the turtles and what he had seen growing up. He said on some occasions, he had helped turtles back to the water, especially if they were tired. Because they came ashore on a low tide, they would sometimes crawl over a hundred yards to build their nest. Sea turtles were made for swimming, not crawling long distances.

Pop and I sat looking at the massive loggerhead as she flipped sand around the nest to camouflage the site. "Look at her eyes," he said. "Most of the time, water comes down their face, just like tears."

Her head was down, her chin resting on the sand. Pop thought the tears were from the ordeal of crawling up the beach, digging her nest, laying the eggs, and then covering and packing it down. The whole process could take two or three hours.

Seeing this event for myself and hearing Pop's explanation made an impression on me, and I said, "Pop, this is amazing. They know what they are doing, don't they?"

"Yep, Mother Nature sure is something That's why our family has always respected animal life. Never abuse wild animals. They are here on earth for us to respect and furnish us with food. Then only use what you need to survive. Remember that always and practice it, you hear me?"

Of course, I said, "Yes sir. I hear you."

When the momma turtle finally made its way to the water and the first wave washed over it, Pop started up the skeeter, and we headed north again. On the way back, he turned on the spotlight mounted on the windshield and aimed the beam on the water's edge. Before we reached Mickler's Pier, we saw a mullet leaping in the air on the incoming tide. The water wasn't very deep there, and we could see a whole school of what Pop called "peter size" mullet. I wasn't sure why he called them peter size mullet. I know my peter wasn't that big, but we caught all we wanted in just one throw of the cast net. He pulled them up on the beach, emptied the net, and I piled them in the number three wash tub.

We were back home around midnight, waking Grandma, who got up to help us with an early breakfast. While Pop knocked the hide off the mullet, Grandma put on the frying pan and began boiling the grits. It wasn't long before we were eating up a storm. Those fresh fried mullet, hot grits, and butter were damn sure good.

Pop hadn't said a word about the three turtle poachers he'd rousted, but I couldn't wait to tell Grandma about our adventure. She listened to my tale and got all upset. Pop looked at me and said, "Now why didn't you just be quiet about all that? Didn't you know it was going to get your Grandma upset?"

"I'm sorry Grandma," I said quickly, "but everything is okay. Please pass the grits and the butter."

Later Pop told me there were other groups of men like we ran into butchering turtles up and down the coast. He said that turtle meat wasn't much different than any other type of meat, but a lot of people thought it was a delicacy, especially people up north where big restaurants served sea turtle soup. He said that's why there's a market for these guys to kill turtles.

Over the years, he said he'd seen turtle shells on the beach, with only their flippers cut out because that was the only meat in the turtle except for its neck. Pop said they had been trying to get some help from the county commissioners and Wildlife Association to hire someone to patrol the beach. He said they had just interviewed Roy Landrum, one of his cousins, for the job, but he hadn't heard if he'd been hired or not. Mr. Landrum would be the first beach patrol person to try and stop the mutilation of turtles.

CONSTABLE ROY LANDRUM

Pop's cousin, Mr. Landrum, got the job. The first time I met Mr. Landrum, Pop and I were frying mullet on a driftwood fire on the beach near the number one artesian well. Pop said, "Looks like we got some company coming. Sure got some strong head lights. About as strong I ever seen."

We watched the lights come up over the high-water dunes, heading in our direction. The buggy was still a half-mile away but moving fast. Pop strolled over to the skeeter. He said nothing, but I knew he wanted to be close to Old Betsy.

As the beach vehicle approached us, its lights dimmed, and the buggy slowed. The driver was sizing us up. When the vehicle was about twenty-five yards away, Pop suddenly said, "I'll be damned. It's that old buzzard cousin of mine in his new beach buggy the county bought him. Roy Landrum in person."

The county buggy rolled up and stopped. The driver yelled out. "Tola, you old fart. How you doin'?"

"Roy, get your butt out and stay a spell. We got some hot fried mullet we cookin' up here. You welcome, we got a plenty."

"Damn Tola, that sounds good, but you got anything to drink like some of your family's shine? I could use a shot of that first."

Pop said, "Just happen to have a jar in my toolbox." Pop opened the toolbox in the back seat and came out with a mason jar wrapped in an old towel. Mr. Landrum took the jar, unscrewed the top, and took a swig. Then to my surprise, which I'd never seen before, he put his head back and gargled the shine before swallowing it.

"Tola, that's damn good shine. I shore thank you. I was getting a little cold in this open buggy in the night air, and that shine already warmed me up a little."

After they talked a bit, Pop said, "Bubba, get Roy some mullet on one them fancy paper plates we got left over from Christmas. Mamie said we had to use them up," he explained to his cousin.

I piled his plate with mullet and grits and listened as he began telling Pop about his job as county constable, patrolling the beach for St. Johns County. He said he wanted to catch the poachers killing the turtles and selling the turtle meat to restaurants.

"Those sons of bitches! Between them and the shrimp boats catching them in their shrimp nets, they going kill off the damn turtles. People just don't have any damn sense about nature and letting nature replenish itself. Only after they can't find a turtle would they understand what the hell they did. Ain't that right Tola?"

Pop said, "Shore as hell you're right enough, Roy."

A loggerhead making her nest on the beach while a hatchling heads to the sea.

FIVE
The Rusty Bolt
"I noticed a strange line in the sand"

Cruising the beach another night, I had my eyes peeled, looking for a turtle crawl. "Pop, there's one," I called out, pointing to the momma turtle's track from the ocean to its nest.

"Yep, shore is." He cut the headlights and slowed, turning the skeeter up toward the high-water dunes as he came to a stop. "Now let's wait a minute or two and let our eyes adjust to the dark."

"But Pop she's up there. Let's go."

"Now dammit, just slow down. That turtle is not like a deer, she ain't going nowhere fast. If she's digging, we could scare her and she'll quit and head back to the water, afraid some animal is after her eggs. We gotta take it slowly and be quiet. If she laying already, she won't stop. I told you this a dozen times before. Don't you remember anything?"

"Sorry Pop. I just excited as the dickens."

"Well, be quiet till we know what's going on, or you'll have to wait in the skeeter."

"Yes sir, I will Pop. Promise."

He looked at me hard for a moment, then turned his head toward the crawl. The moon was full that night, shining like a beacon over the ocean, spotlighting the crawl marks. We climbed out of the skeeter in a few minutes and crept to the turtle crawl. We followed the turtle's trail up the beach on our hands and knees. As we crawled, I noticed a strange line in the sand and touched Pop to call it to his attention. A deep straight line extended along the right side of the crawl, part of the flipper impression in the sand. Pop motioned me to be quiet, and we kept moving slowly toward the dunes.

We stopped by the piles of sand surrounding the nest made by the massive loggerhead sea turtle. I was both amazed and awed by what I saw. The turtle's body contracted, her rear flippers rising off the sand with each contraction. She was laying the last of her eggs. Pop pulled some of the sand pile away so we could see better and shone his shaded flashlight into the pit. The turtle's eggs looked like a large mound of wet ping-pong balls piled together in the deep chamber she'd dug.

As we watched, the turtle released slime from her egg sack onto the top of her eggs. Pop explained that the slime held the heat evenly around the eggs to help them hatch. Pop reached into her egg chamber and brought out a handful of eggs. He did that several times until he had taken about half of them. You might think that's a lot of eggs to poach from the turtle's nest, but a sea turtle lays an average of 110 eggs each time she nests and may nest two or three times a year.

"Where's the sack?" Pop whispered.

I'd forgotten to bring the cloth sack we used to hold the eggs and ran back to the truck to get it. Returning with the sack, we carefully filled it with the eggs.

Pop said, "Let's look for what was making that mark in her flipper."

The turtle was basically in a trance, utterly exhausted after digging the nest and laying her eggs. I eased up toward her head and noticed something sticking out of her right flipper. Pop saw it too—a rusty bolt jammed through the flipper.

I couldn't imagine how this had happened and wondered if it hurt. Pop suggested that she might have gotten it off an old shipwreck while swimming. He reached over and touched it. It appeared to be loose but rusted all the way through. The top of the bolt had a big head, and it was apparent it wouldn't go down through the hole in her flipper. He whispered to me to go to the skeeter and get the bolt cutters from the toolbox.

"We're going to see if we can help her with that thing."

I slipped away, returned to the skeeter, found the bolt cutter, and brought it back to Pop. He glided the jaws of the bolt cutter over the top of her flipper and around the rusty head. With one quick slice, he lopped the head off the rusted bolt.

When he cut the bolt, the turtle moved her flipper, and Pop motioned me to be still. He waited a minute, then slowly dug a hollow from under her flipper to reach the bolt. He eased his hand into the sand, palm up, and took hold of the bolt, moving it around and slowly sliding it out of her flipper.

We both smiled, and the turtle took that flipper and threw a load of sand back towards her hole, spraying us in the process. We laughed out loud, and Pop said, "Why, that's no way to treat us after helping you."

The loggerhead ignored us and went on flipping sand to cover the nest, completely burying her eggs. She gently patted the wet sand on top of the eggs, using the underside of her shell.

I picked up the bag of eggs and started for the skeeter, but Pop wanted us to wait until she finished covering the nest. Afterward, she used her flippers to camouflage the nest by scattering dry sand to conceal the location of her eggs from predators like coons, possums, or foxes.

She took her time and then was ready to return to the sea. Pop wanted to be sure she got back to the water safely. Sea turtles spend most of their life in the water except when they're born or return to lay their eggs. On land, they are awkward and slow. The loggerhead inched along about fifteen to twenty feet, then stopped to rest. The tide had come in since she first crawled ashore and now was at the high-water mark, so she didn't have as far to go. We watched her until she hit the first wave. Then she picked up her pace and plowed into the deep waves, disappearing into her home waters.

I was still a young buck when this event with the turtle and the rusted bolt occurred. Pop and I had raided dozens, if not hundreds, of turtle nests, although we never took more than half the eggs. But this time was special, and I felt a swell of pride knowing we had helped that big mamma turtle. Pop started up the skeeter, and we headed south towards St. Augustine. "Keep your eyes open, Bubba. Let's find another one," he said.

Thinking back on those beach excursions still gives me a thrill. Every trip was an adventure. I loved Pop even when he was upset with me, which happened occasionally, but the old saying applied to Pop—his bark was worse than his bite. Riding the beach was a challenge for Pop, and I experienced the same thing as his passenger and young student. You just never knew what was beyond your headlights. The bottom could fall out from under the tires because of soft sand or wet coquina. In minutes you could be struggling to keep the beach buggy from going down and fighting nature to get up on high ground.

But that didn't happen the night I helped Pop remove a rusty bolt from a sea turtle's flipper.

SIX

Dead Catfish on the Beach
"Bubba come here quick"

Too many surf fishermen had the bad habit of throwing saltwater catfish up on the beach to die, leaving them for seagulls to eat. Some commercial fishermen were guilty of the same thing, and it wasn't uncommon to find a wash tub full of dead catfish laying on the beach. They would toss all of what they called trash fish—saltwater catfish, toadfish, ladyfish, eels, and jellyfish—helping to feed seagulls and other birds and small animals but littering and smelling up the beach for weeks.

They left those carcasses behind, thinking saltwater catfish aren't good to eat. Even Pop called them trash fish because they eat dead fish or other disgusting things in the water. We caught lots of them when seining with the big net, and he would have me dig a hole and bury them. But most people just threw them up on the beach to die. These catfish would lay rotting on the beach for days until only the skeleton remained, with the jagged dorsal fin sticking straight out from the backbone of the catfish.

There are three fins on a dead catfish—and on live ones for that matter—a dorsal fin on top and two pectoral fins on either side of the body. On the tip of each fin is a very sharp stinger filled with nasty toxins. Most catfish stings happen when the fish is flopping around and the fisherman is trying to get the hook out. Sometimes a fisherman might step on the fish to stop it from flopping and gets stung.

Catfish fins were also the enemies of the skeeter's tires. Most of the time, our skeeter's tires were worn bald because we couldn't afford to buy new ones. As you can imagine, catfish fins are bad news for bald tires. We would average at least one or two flat tires per night from catfish fins. Pop would cuss up a blue streak and swear at those damn Yankees for leaving the catfish on the beach every time he had a flat tire. I didn't dare ask him how he knew it was Yankees that left dead catfish on the beach, knowing it would result in a knock on my head, so I kept that thought to myself.

Years later, when I had my own beach buggy, I carried as many as three spare tires with a spare bolted on each side and one on the back.

Even after seagulls and other critters have fed on the dead catfish, they're still dangerous. Hidden in the sand by the incoming tides, they lie in wait like land mines until an unsuspecting person comes along. Beach-lovers stroll the beach hunting for shark's teeth or just for the sheer enjoyment and relaxation of a walk on the beach. But all that changes if they step on a catfish fin hiding in the sand. Sadly, the fins go in easy but are hard to pull out.

And that's where this story begins.

***

Pop and I were fishing one dark, moonless night. We had stopped at a little slough, and he'd caught about fifteen or sixteen mullet with the first cast of his net. He pulled it in and emptied his haul on the beach. He said, "Bubba, I going to run down the beach because those mullets are running to the top of this slough. I want to try and get one more cast in before they head back out to deep water. You bring the skeeter."

I said, "Okay, Pop. As soon as I get these fish in the tub."

As I filled the washtub and hauled it into the skeeter, I heard Pop's blood-curdling scream. Then in a lower voice, he called to me. "Bubba, come here quick. I stepped on one of those god damn catfish, and it's all the ways through my foot."

I jumped in the skeeter, started her up, and drove toward him as quickly as

I could. I grabbed the flashlight, ran over to him, and found him lying down, holding his leg. A dead catfish dangled like a bony shadow below his foot.

His face twisted in pain, Pop yelled as I approached, "Get the whiskey bottle out of the skeeter and the toolbox."

I did as he told me. Setting the toolbox beside him, I handed him the whiskey bottle. He took a big swallow and poured some directly on the puncture wound. I watched his face contort in pain as the liquor splashed over his foot. He gasped and said, "Bubba, open that toolbox fast and get me two pairs of pliers, the cutting pliers and the flat-faced gripping ones."

I searched through the box and found the pliers. Pop took both pliers in one hand and grabbed my arm with the other. He shook me a bit to be sure he had my attention. "Bubba, you gotta help me get this catfish fin out of my foot. You know they've got poison in 'em and I got to get it out now. It's hurting something bad and starting to throb, so you gotta pull that fin up through my foot. First you gotta cut off the fin from the catfish underneath my foot with the cutting pliers."

He instructed me to place the pliers flat against his foot and around the fin to clip the fin from the dead catfish. There were barbs in the spiny fin and pulling it down through his foot would have ripped him up terribly. I raised his foot with the dead catfish hanging down, slid the pliers over the fin flat against the bottom of his foot as he'd instructed, and cut the catfish off.

Pop screamed in pain, but after catching his breath, he said, "Good, son," and lay his foot in the sand.

I could see he was hurting and knew the pain would only get worse when I pulled the fin out. "Pop, I don't think I can pull that fin through your foot. It's going to hurt you too bad. We need to get you to a doctor where he can deaden your foot."

"Bubba, look at me. This thing is hurting worse than anything I've ever had hurt me. The pain isn't going to stop until you get the fin out of my foot. You can do it. You got to do it for me, you hear me?"

"Yes, sir, I hear you," I said in a shaky voice. I took the gripping pliers and moved to his right side, where I could pull the fin straight up and out of his foot. The barb had pushed through the fleshy side of his foot without hitting any bones, thank God.

"Bubba, you take hold of it now and get ready to start pulling. Don't stop pulling till it all the way out, you understand? I going to yell like hell but don't stop till it out. Be sure you got a good hold on it, don't want it to slip out of those pliers."

He urged me to keep pulling even if he passed out from the pain, telling me to keep his face out of the sand until he came to. "Just get that son of bitch out of my foot, please!"

"Hold on a minute, Pop. I'm going to get my T-shirt out of the skeeter to wrap your foot when I get that fin out."

Pop said, "Yeah, that be good, cause it going to bleed a lot when you pull it through, but that's going to help get the poison out. Soak the hole with whiskey before you wrap it in your shirt."

When I was in position with the pliers above the fin, I asked Pop if he was ready. "Yes," he said, "but give me that whiskey bottle." He gulped another swallow before telling me to rip off a piece of my T-shirt. "Going to stuff it in my mouth and bite down on it."

With the cloth in his mouth, he shook his head up and down, signaling me to go ahead. "Okay, Pop, you ready?" I asked.

He nodded again. Pop was lying on his side, so I extended his leg slowly to put my knee on his leg just above his hurt foot. I gripped the fin in the pliers, thinking, *Oh God, let me do this right and come straight up and out with that damn fin.*

When I clamped down on the fin, Pop let out a groan. I pulled the fin out, and he screamed. Blood poured from the wound. Pop spit out the rag and lay back in the sand, his head on his arm. His groaning stopped, and he grew quiet. I eased his foot up and wrapped it with my T-shirt, and poured some whiskey on it to help kill any infection. I got his pants out of the skeeter, rolled them up, and placed them under his head.

After retrieving the net and all our gear, I cleaned off the back seat for him to lay down. I kneeled beside him. He was breathing hard and exhausted from the pain. "Pop, can you get up?" I asked him. "I'll help you into the back seat, and we can go home."

He smiled at me with tears in his eyes. "Bubba, you did good here, son, as good as any grown man. Thank you for being the best beach partner I have ever had. You can help me into the back seat, but watch out for that foot."

After a while, Pop told me, "The pain has already started to ease up. I knew it would soon we got that damn fin out. Take us home. I'm going to be just fine thanks to you, Bubba."

I slid behind the wheel of the skeeter, cranked her up, and drove north through the Graveyard. When I hit the soft spots, I shoved it into second gear and steered toward the dunes, stomping the gas and plowing through those soft spots. I'd seen Pop do this a thousand times and never guessed I would be doing the same under these circumstances. I got to Mickler's Pier, told Pop to hold on, and started up over the sand dunes.

Pop said, "Give her the gas, Bubba, and stay in the old ruts."

I barreled up through the dunes and onto the hard road heading for home. I was one happy and proud nine-year-old boy, but I sure had grown up some that night. When we got home, Grandma doctored Pop's foot. She heated a pot of water on the stove and added a whole jar of salt. He soaked his foot in the hot salty water for a half-hour, and then Grandma dried his foot and swabbed the wound with iodine.

Pop kept saying he was all right, but we could see he was exhausted and still hurting. Grandma gave Pop four aspirin and put him in bed. The next day we took him to see Dr. Roberts, who gave him a tetanus shot. Pop told the doctor how it happened and how I had cut the fin and pulled it out. I think Dr. Roberts was impressed with the job I'd done. After bandaging Pop's foot, he said, "It's a good thing you got that fin out of his foot before the poison set in." Then that old doctor began laughing.

"What's so funny?" Pop asked him.

"I was just thinking it was a shame you had to waste all that whiskey Tola, but it helped kill any germs and wash out the poison."

Before we left, the doctor told Pop to stay off his foot for a few days. Sure enough, in a week, he was up and around again. Pop later told me a story about one of his brothers who stepped on a catfish fin that went through his big toe. It got infected, and they thought they'd have to cut his toe off, maybe even his foot. But thank the Lord they only removed half of the fleshy side of his big toe on the right foot.

After hearing that story, I was mighty grateful that Pop came through the catfish ordeal as well as he did. But I learned something important that night that has always stayed with me. And that is, we sometimes must do things we may not want or even think we're capable of doing, but we do them anyway because we don't have a choice. As a nine-year-old child, I was pushed into that corner because Pop's situation forced me to be strong and helped me grow into a more confident, independent man.

When it came to raising my children, I sometimes remembered the swirl of emotions I felt as I gripped that catfish fin and yanked it out of Pop's foot. I still remember how good I felt after it was over, and Pop had complimented me on how I'd performed that night on the beach. I used this experience as a training tool for myself and to help me nurture and encourage my children.

Hopefully, other people reading this book have had similar experiences. If that's the case, you know what I'm talking about and have used your own "catfish fin" experience to become a better person. I know it helped me, and I'll never forget it.

SEVEN
More True Adventures on the Beach

THE SEA MONSTER

"What in God's name is it, Pop?" I screamed at my step-grandfather, who was driving the skeeter along the beach one night. "It's a big black sea monster. Stop quick, Pop!" I begged him.

I was staring at a big black thing as tall as a five-story building, and it was moving slowly, coming right at us. I'd never been so scared in my whole life.

Pop wheeled the buggy toward the dunes and stomped down on the gas. I didn't know what kind of creature it was and was afraid it would get us before we could escape. I ducked down on the floorboard as far as I could go, expecting the worst thing in the world was fixing to happen.

It was one of those moonless and cloudy nights. And we were in the Graveyard to boot. Everything went quiet. I couldn't see a thing from my position on the floorboards with my eyes squeezed shut. I was busy praying, but I had to wonder why Pop had stopped. Did the monster have us?

Then Pop laughed and said, "It's okay, Bubba. You can come up out of that hole and see what we got."

I was shaking so bad I could hardly move and didn't want to move. But Pop kept after me, and I finally peeped out.

"Look," he said. "It's a big old oil tanker that must have broken loose from its towing ship and is now aground here on the beach." The ship was slowly rolling back and forth as the waves washed against it, giving me the impression it was a monster moving in our direction.

When we got to St. Augustine, Pop stopped at a pay phone and called the police department. He told them about the stranded ship so they could report it to the Coast Guard, giving them the approximate location on the beach. We returned to the stranded vessel to find a Coast Guard truck with flashing lights. They had already contacted the crew members on the tanker.

We returned the next day and watched them trying to refloat the tanker and get it off the beach. They had to wait until high tide to break it loose and start moving it out to sea. I was glad to see the monster gone. It had scared the hell out of me.

Life on the beach was a series of never-ending, constantly changing adventures. My father died when I was only seven years old, and Pop became my surrogate father. Together we roamed the beaches of northeast Florida, and he taught me more about life and nature than any book could have. Here are more of my childhood adventures.

DOLPHINS IN THE NET

One night I accompanied Pop and his family as they fished with a long seine net. It was well after dark, and everyone was tired and ready to go home when Pop said, "Let's seine this slough to the end and go home."

No one argued with him.

They put the net in at the beginning of the pocket, usually the deep end, and started moving toward the far side. Just then, something hit the net, and Uncle Charlie hollered, "We got something damn big in here."

The water churned and splashed like all hell had broken loose. Pop yelled, "There's some dolphins ahead of the net, but I don't think there's a problem because they are moving towards the end of the slough and will swim out to deep water before we pull out the net."

This kind of thing had happened before with schools of sharks, dolphins, and even stingrays. Ninety percent of the time, they swam out of the net before we pulled it in. But this time, one dolphin decided to head right back against the net and smashed into it. He started twisting and turning and soon had become tangled in the net. We could see that it was a baby dolphin and realized it was so young it didn't understand it should have stayed with the school of adult dolphins running ahead of the net, which would have taken it out of the slough.

Big momma dolphin decided to swim to the rescue. She rammed right into the net next to the baby dolphin but backed off before getting tangled in it. She was smart enough to know the little one was trapped in the net. Instead, she began circling the slough, watching and waiting.

Seeing the situation, the men decided to pull the little fellow up on the beach and get him out. Even though it was a baby, the dolphin is a big fish, and it fought as though its life depended on it. I can hardly blame him. He didn't know they were trying to save him. At that point, the only thing to do was let him keep thrashing around and hope he'd tire himself out and stop fighting. When he did calm down, they slowly untangled him and pulled him back into the water.

An unusual thing happened after they released the baby dolphin in the surf. Big Momma Dolphin, still circling near us, popped her head out of the water and made a series of squawking and whistling sounds, almost like she was thanking us. Then she rushed to the little guy, and he went right up beside her, and together they swam toward the open end of the net and the slough before slipping away to deep water. The little guy stayed right next to her.

The men pulled the net out and hauled in a mess of mullet and small reds. Now it was my turn to go to work instead of watching the fun. We filled two-and-a-half wash tubs with the fish, and I remember thinking could this young boy's life get any better?

EIGHT
Sharks & Mullet Don't Mix
"It was an unbelievable sight"

One night during the summer, I believe it was 1942, Pop and I had driven to Vilano Beach and hadn't seen a single mullet or any turtle crawls. So we turned around and headed back north toward home, thinking that this would probably be one of those dry runs where we didn't catch anything. Pop was prepared to cook up a batch of mullet. He'd brought his blow pot frying pan, grease, and cornmeal. If we caught any fish, we were going to clean and eat them right there on the beach.

We had the spotlight aimed at the water as we were driving along. My job was to watch the water to see if any mullet jumped when the light hit the water. Pop's job was to drive and keep his eyes open for washouts, sloughs, soft bottoms, and wet coquina. We had been doing this all evening, searching for schools of mullet. Pop kept asking me if I had seen anything yet. I know he did it to be sure I was still paying attention to the light on the water.

Suddenly, the light hit a little slough, and I spotted mullet jumping. I yelled out, "Mullet, Pops! Mullet on the beach."

Pop reached up, cut the light off, and turned the skeeter toward the hill. He jumped out, grabbed his cast net, and hurried down to the water. I hauled the wash tub from the back and followed Pop, watching as he prepared to cast his net. It takes a lot of practice to throw a cast net well. It involves a combination of motions from looping and cinching the hand line over your wrist, coiling the line, and bunching the net's fabric, gripping a section in your teeth, and rotating your shoulders and hips to toss and spread the net into the water.

Pop made it look easy.

He threw a perfectly rounded, flat circle into what looked like a foot of water. His net came alive. Mullet were jumping everywhere. I'd never seen so many in one spot in my young life. Pop tried to pull the loaded net up on the beach and yelled for me to give him a hand. His net was slammed full of fish. That night he caught 175 fish in a single throw. That was the most mullet he had ever caught in one cast. It almost filled the number three washtub.

Pop said that's enough for tonight. "We got more fish than we can clean and eat and the rest we'll put in the cooler with the ice and take home."

We drove over the dunes to the second well, where we could get clean water to clean the fish. I'd wash them, and Pop would butcher them. We cleaned all we thought we could eat and put the rest in the cooler with the ice. He left the clean fish on the top in a plastic bag, and we headed back to the beach.

I asked Pop to stop when we found that slough where all those mullet were for just a few minutes. I wanted to shine the spotlight on them and see if they were still in there as thick as they were.

He said okay, "but we can't shine that light very long with the motor off, because it will run down the battery. Then I will have to get the crank out and crank the motor by hand and I don't feel like doing that tonight."

Pop drove high on the soft white sand next to the dunes before returning to where we had caught the mullet. He pointed to an old log and said we might as well build a fire right here. "Get the pot, and I'll cook up some fish, and you can look at that slough for a while with the spotlight, but again not too damn long to save the battery."

Before I could run off, he added, "But first gather some driftwood for our fire then get the cleaned fish in the bag out and the fish meal and the oil out of the skeeter."

I kept saying "Yes sir" as he gave me instructions. Next, he told me to lay the cleaned fish on the top of the cooler and salt and pepper them.

"I'll fix the cornmeal bag and take it from there," he said.

After helping Pop get ready to fry the fish, I climbed into the skeeter and turned the spotlight on the slough where we had just caught the mullet. It looked like thousands were jumping in all directions. Then I saw the backs of some big animals with great big fins sticking out of the water. Sharks! There must've been eight or ten of them mixing it up with the mullet. They had chased the mullet up into that slough and blocked them off so they couldn't get out. They had themselves a feast.

I called Pop, "You ain't going to believe this. Look at all the sharks in that slough."

Three or four sharks had to be twelve to fifteen feet long. They glided along in the shallow water, splashing mullet in the air. One giant shark chased a mullet toward the shore until it was almost entirely out of the water. He flipped around and finally got back into deeper water to swim away. What an unbelievable sight! Right there in front of us was a spectacular show of nature.

Pop said, "Well I'll be damned to hell and back. I ain't never seen anything like this before in all my fishing days. I'll tell you one damn thing, I'm sure going to be careful in the future before I go out in that water at nighttime. That's the damnedest thing I've ever seen."

That's why this was the only place we saw any mullet all night long, and if it hadn't been for those sharks driving them up into that slough, we wouldn't have seen any. I cut the light off, and we went to frying fish. We ate nothing but fried mullet and bread, and boy, were they good. I ate a dozen fish by myself.

Pop said, "Bubba, you know, we got all those fish in the cooler to take home and sell on the hill. Best we take care of them so as not to run out of ice. It's about 10 o'clock, we can be home in about an hour. Let's go home and sleep in our own beds and not be laying around in this sand tonight. I'll pour out that grease and put the blow pot away. You put out that fire good, won't hurt nothin' leave red coals, nothing but sand around. You clean off the cooler and put those paper plates and bread away and we'll get ready to go."

"Pop you said earlier that you might let me drive home tonight," I reminded him. "Can I, please Pop? I'll drive real good."

"Okay, you can drive us, but you have to be on your toes driving through the Graveyard. We don't want to get stuck, so damn well watch what the hell you are doing."

We only hit a couple of bad spots going home. One of them was in the Graveyard. It was wet coquina that had no bottom. I hit it going about 35 miles an hour, and as soon as I felt those front tires sinking, I turned towards the dunes and slapped it into second gear.

Pop yelled, "Give it all the gas to the floor and head to the high-water hills," and I did. The front tires pulled up out of the wet coquina just in time. We were starting to drag on the bottom of the skeeter frame.

That's the kind of driving I learned from the early age of seven- or eight years old, riding next to Pop when he would go through those bad stretches of beach. After a while, it's all automatic, knowing what to do in those dangerous spots of coquina.

Running as late as we were, Pop told me to go to Barney's, hit the highway, and take us home. God knows those nights on the beach were exciting for me. Pop loved the challenges, and I was becoming his backup. He loved teaching me and seeing me drive the skeeter at such a young age.

By the time I was twelve to fourteen, I could climb into almost any car stuck in soft sand and drive it off the beach or to hard ground. It was all thanks to my training riding with Pop, who taught me what to do when those danger spots came up — dig out in front and back of the stuck car's tires. Let out about half of the air in the tires, so it was soft and flat enough to stay on top of the sand. Now get in and rock the car back and forth, packing down the sand. Do not spin the tires; that will only dig the tire in deeper. Gradually you eased back and forth to hard ground, or you have made hard pan tracks for ten to twenty feet. You go as fast as you can without spinning the tires at that point, and out you come.

Knowing how to rescue cars stuck in the sand was worth many a $20 bill from the grateful owners of those cars. A car stuck in the water was an entirely different matter. They mainly had to be pulled out by us with the skeeter. If the tide was washing over the vehicle, we'd get Uncle Barney with his wrecker. We saw quite a few cars that the ocean took. People were not paying attention to the tide coming in, and parked near the water. Some even drove into the water. Crazy!

NINE
The Cockfight
"I remember being very scared"

After my father died, Pop took me almost everywhere with him, including to a cockfight. That experience was both exciting and frightening, as you can imagine since I was only seven years old. Pop and my father had been spectators at many cockfights, and I believe Pop thought I'd have a better understanding of the Minorcan culture by attending a cockfight.

Cockfighting is a sport dating back to ancient times in Greece, Italy, and other countries. So, it was understandable that it was popular with the Spanish and Minorcans in Florida. Cockfighting was called a "blood sport" and had already been outlawed in Florida and other states when Pop took me, but that didn't stop people from holding cockfights or attending them. The law said it was a cruel and bloody sport. And it was. The roosters usually fought for their lives until one was dead. Because it was illegal, the handlers and the sponsors moved the fights around to different places, and word quickly spread among the cockfighting crowd. This strategy kept them ahead of the law, at least most of the time.

There was a good reason why the fights were so popular, even though they were against the law, and people could go to jail if arrested. And that reason was MONEY. A lot of money was made and lost at these fights, with all the spectators betting on which rooster would survive the bout, meaning it was the last one left standing.

Farmers and handlers bred the gamecocks to be aggressive. The bloody sport was made even bloodier by attaching metal spurs to the cock's natural spurs. These sharpened steel spurs were at least three inches long and deadly.

They fought in a round pit called a cockpit, and the fight was to the death or until one of them couldn't stand anymore. While all this craziness was going on, people were cheering and placing bets on how long one rooster would last over the other and who would win. Even if the wounded rooster would get up. It was a cruel sport, but it was a sport handed down from generation-to-generation Pop said. He said there were cockfights even before Jesus was born.

When my grandmother Mamie learned that Pop planned to take me to the cockfight, they had a big fight. He finally stomped out of the house, dragging me along and telling Grandma he was taking me with him, and that was that.

I don't remember exactly where we went, but it was at a farm near Green Cove Springs on Pacetti Highway—State Road 16—or at Moccasin Branch. I remember the roosters fought in a big barn with milk cows stabled around the cockpit. At one point, they stopped the fight, and the strangest thing happened — the handler put his mouth on the neck of the rooster near its head. It looked like he was kissing the bird, and I asked Pop what he was doing.

Pop said, "That roosters lost a lot of blood, and the handler is trying to pull what blood he has up to the rooster's head so he can stay alive and keep fighting until he either drops or he sticks his steel spur through the other cock's head or his heart and kills him."

During the fight, one of the milk cows became frightened by all the noise and started kicking the walls in her stall. She was making a heck of a racket, and people were screaming. Pop backed me into a corner of the barn and shielded me from the screaming people. I remember being very scared with all the people hollering and the cows and horses bellowing. It was suddenly a panic.

Three men tried to calm the frightened cow doing most of the kicking and bellowing, but this only made her crazier. They finally fastened ropes on her head and horns and told everyone to get out of the way. They pulled her toward the open barn door, but when she reached the door, she bolted out. The man who owned the farm hollered at the men holding the ropes to let her go.

"She ain't going far," the farmer said. "She can't get out the fence and the gate is closed."

The frightened cow charged into the barnyard dragging the three ropes behind her, yowling like the devil was after her. They closed the barn doors and returned to the cockpit as if nothing had happened. But for me, wow! That was something.

When Grandma heard about the panicked cow and how frightened I was, she tore into Pop. Grandma usually got her way, and that was the first and last rooster fight I attended with Pop.

I remember him telling her, "Well, he's got to grow up someday. But the hell with cockfights if I have to listen to this shit every time I take him."

TEN
The War Hits Home
"I could see fire on the water"

World War II impacted those of us living in northeast Florida like the rest of the nation. Our entry into the war began when the Japanese attacked Pearl Harbor on December 7, 1941, followed by Germany declaring war against us. Between 1940 and 1947, more than 250,000 Floridians served in the armed forces, including Pop.

When war broke out, I was only six years old, but I remember our family enduring tough times. They only got worse after Pop was drafted. We saw the effects of the war all around us. The Coast Guard and the Civil Defense patrolled the beaches and watched the skies for enemy planes. Curiously, two incidents happened on our beach during this period, and I was there to observe some of the drama.

GERMAN SUB SINKS TANKER

It's late on a Friday night, and Inkey's is packed with folks looking for a good time and a chance to get away from their ordinary lives for a few hours. Inkey's was an oceanfront bar and dance hall at the end of 16th Avenue South in Jacksonville Beach. We often used their ramp leading down to the beach to begin our nightly beach excursions, searching for turtle crawls and mullet.

Pearl Clark and Lester Harrison owned Inkey's, but the neighborhood hangout was only there for a few years before the name changed to the Ocean

View Restaurant. Today, a condo unit called South Shore is sitting in its place.

Nothing stays the same, but on that night of April 10, 1942, I tagged along with Pop, grandma, and my mother to Inkey's, where they liked to sit and drink beer. While they partied with their friends, I would go down and play in the sand. Later, exhausted from playing, I returned to Inkey's and fell asleep in one of the booths. Mother draped her sweater over me to keep me warm. People were talking and dancing. The jukebox was blaring, but I slept through it all until later that night when the sounds of people yelling and running toward the beach woke me. We joined the rush to see what was going on. Pop held onto me to be sure the crowd didn't knock me over. Outside, he pointed toward the dark horizon. In the distance, I could see fire on the water. Suddenly, an explosion sent a giant ball of flame into the air, followed by several smaller blasts.

I had no idea what was going on. I asked Pop, and he explained, "A German submarine has torpedoed an American oil tanker and is trying to sink it."

Then we heard rapid gunshots and Pop said, "That's the Germans shooting at the men on the sinking tanker."

Everyone was frightened to see such a spectacle, and it brought the war home to the hundreds of people watching this tragedy unfold before our eyes Because it was a Friday night, the Jacksonville Beach Boardwalk, with its carnival rides and honky-tonk joints, was crowded. I was not quite seven years old and didn't understand what it meant, but I knew it was something awful. We couldn't take our eyes off that terrible scene, watching the burning tanker and wondering what must have happened to the crew members.

The next morning Pop took Grandma and me to the 16th Avenue ramp, where we could see remnants of the doomed tanker floating, smoke, and flames still visible from the shore. I later learned the tanker was the SS *Gulf America* on its maiden voyage from Port Arthur, Texas, to New York, carrying over 100,000 barrels of fuel oil. She was traveling unescorted along the coast of Florida, and the ship's captain was not employing the traditional zigzag maneuvers usually used to avoid torpedo attacks as she cruised almost five miles offshore. Perhaps the tanker's captain thought he was safe since he was so close to shore, but he didn't know that German U-boat 123 had followed him since the tanker passed St. Augustine.

At 10:10 p.m., 28-year-old U-boat commander Reinhard Hardegen ordered the submarine brought up to periscope depth. As he peered through the eyepiece of the periscope, Hardegen could scarcely believe his good luck. The Jacksonville Beach Boardwalk was lit up like a Christmas tree, and he saw the tanker standing out against the bright lights of the beach community.

In a 1992 interview with *The Baltimore Sun*, the elderly German captain—he was 79 at the time—vividly recalled the night he sunk the tanker.

"There was no blackout. I could see the big wheel (the Ferris wheel) in the amusement park and all the lights and the motorcars in full light. It was very easy for me," he said. "I could see the ship silhouetted against the lights."

Good luck for the German captain, but bad luck for the tanker and the United States since we needed that oil for the war effort. As we stood staring out to sea that night, everyone talked about how close the Germans were and speculated that they could be coming ashore at any time and shooting us.

I didn't know anything about the war at my age, but I felt the fear of everyone around me. Pop kept telling me. "It's okay, Bubba, we have Coast Guard up and down the beach patrolling and the German Army is a long way from us across the ocean."

That may have been true at the time, but as we'd learn in only a few short months, the Germans were not content to stay in Europe, and they'd send spies onto the beach I loved.

ELEVEN
Nazi Spies on Our Beach
"The men motioned for us to stop"

Late one night in June of 1942, Pop and I were cruising down the beach in his skeeter on our way home after catching a load of mullet. We'd driven south toward St. Augustine to the second well and filled a wash tub with the fish.

Pop had made me a cast net, and it was my first chance to use it. It takes real skill to make one of these nets, but it's a skill Pop had learned, probably from his father. A cast net is round with small weights along the edges. You need both hands to throw and spread it open in the water.

My net was about four feet across, and I was only about four feet tall, but I could stretch it out and throw it open pretty good for a seven-year-old kid. Pop gave me several lessons after he made it and I practiced tossing that net repeatedly. I wasn't as good as Pop, who could make his net sing, but remember, I was just a kid and still learning the art of casting a net.

That night, I used my net to catch my first mullet and a prouder boy you'd never seen. I think Pop was proud of me too. Neither of us knew it at the time, but Pop's best friend, my father, would be dead in another month, and Pop would take over as my surrogate father. After filling our tub with mullet, we drove north toward Jacksonville Beach, past the Graveyard, and were approaching the old Mickler's Pier when a bunch of bright lights hit us. Squinting ahead, we saw four or five men silhouetted in our headlights. They carried large flashlights, and they were all pointed at us. Pop may have been worried, but he didn't show it. As for me, my heart felt like it was trying to beat its way out of my chest.

As Pop slowed, a couple of the men stepped directly in our path, and we could see they wore uniforms and had rifles slung across their backs. At least they'd only pointed their flashlights at us, not the rifles. The men motioned for us to stop, and Pop did as directed. He turned off the headlights but kept the parking lights on so we could see.

One of the men came up to Pop and asked to see his driver's license. Pop was wearing his old fishing shorts and told the man, "It's in my pants in the back seat." Pop started to reach back, but the man motioned him to stop and said, "I'll get your pants. You just stay still."

He found Pop's wallet and pulled out the driver's license. After reviewing it closely for a minute, he looked at Pop and asked, "Where you headed?"

I didn't feel like we were in danger because the man acted like a cop, although I knew he wasn't wearing a police uniform. I also knew we hadn't done anything wrong.

Pop told him we were on our way home to Jacksonville Beach. "You can see the address on my driver's license," he said.

The officer looked again and said, "Okay, but you can't go any further north on the beach tonight. You need to turn around and go back south to get off the beach."

Pop remained calm, even though he must have been boiling inside thinking about having to drive twenty miles in the opposite direction of our home. He said, "Do you mind telling me what this is all about and who you are?"

The uniformed man didn't seem to mind the question. He was a big man with a rifle accompanied by three other serious-looking men also carrying rifles. He stared from Pop to me and back at Pop before answering. "Sir," he said, "I am a sergeant with the United States Coast Guard. We have orders to block all the traffic on the beach from Mickler's Pier to Ponte Vedra Beach. We are supporting U.S. Special Agents about a possible German spy operation landing on this beach."

Our country was at war with the Germans. One of their submarines had torpedoed a U.S. tanker right off Jacksonville Beach only two months earlier. And now they were landing spies on our beaches? Can you imagine how this surprising news might have affected me?

Pop politely thanked him for the news, then asked the sergeant, "How about letting us continue right here on the Pier Trail Road? We can drive over the sand dunes to the hard road. Otherwise, it's fifteen to twenty miles back south before I can get up on A1A."

The officer considered that and then told us to wait a minute. He stepped away and got out his Walkie-Talkie. We couldn't hear what he was saying, but he must have been explaining the situation to his superior officer. In a minute, he came back and said, "Okay, but I have to ride with you in the back seat." He called to the other uniformed men telling them to hold their ground until he returned.

With the sergeant watching from the back seat, Pop turned the skeeter around and edged his way toward the dunes. He immediately found the Mickler Trail going through the dunes up to A1A. We saw more Coast Guardsmen blocking the road when we hit the highway. The sergeant got out of the backseat and walked over to talk to the one in charge. This man was just as serious as the sergeant and gave us a hard look before nodding and ordering the other men to move the barricades.

As we drove home, Pop said he would call Roy in the morning and see if he could find out what was happening. Mr. Roy Landrum, as you learned in an earlier chapter, was a St. Johns County Constable who patrolled the beach. Roy was also Pop's cousin.

Pop called him the next day, and Roy said he couldn't get into all the details, but it concerned some German spies who had come ashore from a German submarine. "As soon as the government releases the story and it goes public, I'll tell you everything I know," he said.

We learned more about the German saboteurs that landed on Ponte Vedra Beach in a few days. But there was much more to the story, as we would later learn. The landing on our beach was part of a German plot to blow up defense plants, railroad lines, and water supplies to create panic and damage our country's ability to manufacture war materiel. Hitler wanted to show Americans they were not safe even with the Atlantic Ocean between Europe and the USA.

The German Fuehrer had personally approved what they called Operation Pastorius, and it involved two teams of highly trained, English-speaking spies. The first four-man unit came ashore on a Long Island beach four days before the landing in Ponte Vedra Beach. They buried their explosives and the German uniforms they wore and changed into civilian clothes. Before they made their get-away, however, a patrolling Coast Guardsman approached and questioned the men. They offered him a bribe to forget he had seen them, and he became even more suspicious but pretended to play along since he was unarmed. The four men left the beach, and the Coast Guardsman immediately reported the incident to headquarters, but by the time the search patrol arrived, the saboteurs had reached a railroad station and had taken a train to New York City.

In Ponte Vedra Beach, the four Nazi agents rafted ashore and buried waterproof boxes of explosives and money in the sand. But here's the crazy part: After they had buried the boxes, they made their way to the combination post office, store, service station, and icehouse owned by Alice and Roy Landrum. That's right, Pop's cousin and his wife owned the store, and Mrs. Landrum was the Ponte Vedra-Palm Valley postmaster at the time. I doubt if Mr. Landrum knew that his wife had spoken to one of the Germans, but she would later tell the authorities that one of the men came inside the store and asked about the bus schedule to Jacksonville. The other three waited outside, and when the bus arrived, they climbed aboard and departed. They ended up in Jacksonville, where they checked into two different downtown hotels. The next day they caught a train to Cincinnati and split up, two going to Chicago and the other two to New York.

It all sounds like a good plan, doesn't it? But the entire operation fell apart when the leader of the New York group chickened out and called the FBI. In the end, authorities recovered all the explosives and captured the eight men. They were tried and convicted within two months, and six of the spies were electrocuted. The other two cooperating Germans received lengthy prison sentences.

The news of what the Germans had planned and that Pop and I were on the beach not long after they came ashore put a scare into us. The war was more real than ever—our German enemy had invaded our beach.

Ponte Vedra Beach sign recognizing Operation Pastorius and the landing of Nazi spies during World War II.

TWELVE
Hunting Season
"You need to eat every one of them"

Pop made it plain that he and all his family did not kill animals just to be killing them. He taught me survival skills and the correct way to treat nature and all her creatures. God put the animals here to feed us, he would tell us, so whatever you killed, you ate.

I learned that lesson when I was about seven years old and got a BB gun for Christmas. Acres of piney woods and scrublands surrounded our house, and I recall a wildfire sweeping through the woods. There was nothing left but black ashes as far as you could see. But it didn't take long before little green sprouts poked up through the ash as grass, weeds, and even the palmetto plants came back to life.

The return of the vegetation attracted flocks of quail and robins feasting on the young plants and the worms and insects that had survived the fire. Seeing all those birds excited me, and with my trusty BB gun in hand, I crawled across the blackened fields and took aim at a flock of robins. I must have killed a dozen of them, and I thought Pop would be proud of me.

Boy, was I wrong! He asked me what I intended to do with all those dead birds. I hadn't given it much thought, but I figured I'd dig a hole and bury them. When I told Pop my plan, he said, "No sir, you're going to clean the feathers off them, and I'll show you how to butcher them and clean out the guts. Then your grandmother will fry them for you. You need to eat every one of them. You got that? If you want to shoot something, put up a damn target and shoot at that."

That taught me never to shoot anything I didn't intend to eat, and never again did I kill anything just to shoot harmless animals. But eating the robins wasn't the end of my lesson. I also had to wash my filthy ash-covered clothes and accept the severe tongue-lashing Grandma gave me. That was not a good day for me, but it taught me some important lessons about respecting our animals.

THIRTEEN
Hunting Dogs Ain't Pets
"The poor thing was struggling to breathe"

Happy and Queenie were two of our hunting dogs. They were siblings, and we used them to tree coons, jump deer and hogs, and other animals. Pop had certain rules about his dogs and would say, "Don't play with the hunting dogs." He didn't want me to treat them like pets and advised, "It's not good to get close to any animal because it hurts real bad if you lose them." He said dogs and other pets get sick, and you have to take their lives to put them out of their misery.

Well, I couldn't help myself. I liked Happy a lot. No, I loved Happy. He would rub against my leg and lick my hand when I fed him. But not Queenie. She would growl if I came too close to her when she was eating. Pop would catch me petting Happy and say, "Okay, I warned you. You will have to learn the hard way."

Pop and I had the dogs with us one morning to go squirrel hunting. Happy and Queenie were in their pens in the back of the truck as we headed to Twelve Mile Swamp. We brought the dogs just in case we saw a deer or hog on the way. Usually, though, they stayed in their pens on the truck. But things were about to change.

As we approached the tramp road going into the swamp, four or five hogs dashed from the bushes in front of us and ran down the road toward the swamp. Pop pulled the truck into the bushes and jumped out with his shotgun. He yelled for me to turn the dogs loose on the hogs, and I did.

"Come on boy," he said to me, "don't stand there like a bump on a log. Get your gun and let's get us a hog. I can taste those fried pork chops already. I'm tired of eating squirrel every night."

The dogs were singing out right away because they could smell those hogs, and they chased after them. Before they reached the swamp, they stopped and began baying at a big bunch of palmettos. They were snarling, barking, and growling something fierce as they ran back and forth around the clump of palmetto bushes.

Pop watched the dogs for a moment and said, "Hold up, Bubba. There's something bad those dogs don't like in the palmettos."

Seeing us behind them, the dogs must have felt braver because they charged into the thick clump of palmetto bushes. But not for long. Queenie leaped out just as fast as she had entered. The hair on the back of her neck was standing up, and she was growling and barking. We could hear Happy snarling and growling, telling us he was still after some critter. Then we heard a loud "Yip," and I knew something terible had happened to my beloved hound dog.

About that time, a huge black boar hog emerges from the bushes with bloody tusks sticking out both sides of his mouth. Pop didn't hesitate and pumped a load of buckshot in that old rascal, blowing half his head off. Even mortally wounded, the hog ran around in circles for two or three minutes before he fell over dead. Pop said he must have been way ahead of his herd before we came along.

I didn't care about the dead hog and dashed into the palmettos looking for Happy. Pop yelled at me not to go in there, but I had to find my dog. I found Happy lying down with his whole side ripped open and his guts hanging out. "Pop, come quick," I screamed. "Happy is hurt. He needs our help."

Pop came through the bushes, and when he saw Happy, he said, "Damn, that big bastard killed Happy."

"No, Pop," I cried, "Happy's still breathing, we got to help him."

Pop looked from Happy to me and shook his head. "I'm sorry, Bubba, there's only one way we can help Happy now."

I put my hand close to the dog's head to pet him. Happy raised his head, stared into my eyes, and licked my hand. Then he laid his head back and closed his eyes. The poor thing was struggling to breathe. It was almost more than I could bear to watch him suffer.

Pop said, "Well, son, you going to do it, or do you want me to put him out of his misery?"

"Please don't do it yet, Pop."

"We have to. If you really care about him suffering like he is and hurting so bad, then we have to. We don't have any other choice."

"I can't do it Pop. Please."

"Okay, son. You get out of here and I will be out in a minute."

I walked away bawling something awful. The first thing I saw was the boar's body. Fury overcame my sorrow, and all I could think was this was the monster that had ripped Happy open. I kicked the dead hog with all the strength in my little body. When I heard the blast from Pop's shotgun, I flopped to the ground and cried some more.

When Pop came out, he sat down next to me. He put his arm around me and said, "Now you know why I told you not to get close to our dogs like they were your pets. It hurts real bad, don't it son? In this life, there are times when your mind has got to overrule your heart, and this was one of those times. We had to think of putting Happy out of his misery. I hope you don't have many more of these times, but I'm afraid you will."

I was still sobbing, thinking about poor Happy, when Pop gave me a little hug to let me know the lecture was over. He added, "Life goes on. Let's get this big bastard hog back to camp. We'll butcher him up and eat on him. We'll get the last laugh for Happy. Queenie will feast on the scraps from that son of a bitch, too!

Queenie birthed a set of five pups the following year, fathered by Uncle

Charlie's redbone coonhound. We kept two littermates, a brother and sister, naming the male puppy Happy and the female Queen B after her mother.

The following year, Queenie came down with distemper, similar to pneumonia in people. She got so sick she couldn't stand up or move from the bed box in her pen. So here we go again. I dreaded what I had to do, but I did it. We buried Queenie and put a little cross on her grave with the words, *Here lies Queenie. The grave of a good hunting dog. Thanks for the puppies you gave us.*

I stayed away from having dogs or pets until we moved into our house on the river with its sprawling yard. The children wanted dogs for pets, and I gave in and bought them two German shepherds they named Caesar and Queenie. They were great guard dogs. You didn't dare get out of your car unless you were family or a family member was with the dogs.

One day a terrible accident occurred. Caesar loved to chase the cars coming into our yard and somehow became jammed between the gate post and the car's front wheel. The poor thing suffered terrible internal and external injuries, and we had to put him out of his misery. We buried Caesar by his pen on the hill next to the barn.

Every time something like that happened, it felt like a piece of me died.

Missing Caesar, I brought home an Alaskan Malamute puppy we named Klondike. He grew into a beautiful dog with black, white, and brown fur and deep blue eyes. He looked just like the dogs pulling the sleds in Alaska.

Time marched on. All my children left home, and I went through a divorce. No one was at home during the day except Klondike, who I allowed to run free in our big yard since I didn't want to pen him up or chain him. That turned out to be a bad mistake.

Klondike roamed the neighborhood, making friends wherever he went. But he was always waiting for me at the end of the day. When he saw my truck coming, he'd race me home. I looked forward to seeing him galloping alongside me, feeling my heart swell seeing this magnificent animal I'd raised from a pup. I didn't realize that other people might prize my big, beautiful dog.

One day I drove home, and there was no Klondike racing after me. I drove around the neighborhood, calling for him, but no one had seen him. I searched for days but finally accepted that Klondike was gone for good. In my misery, I realized that I'd failed Klondike. He had loved me, and I loved him just as much, but it was my job to protect him, and I had let him down. The thoughts of my failure brought a load of guilt and pain that remained with me for a long time.

After I lost Klondike, I decided I couldn't take any more hurt like that. Life is too short. Putting your pets out of their misery or losing them caused too much grief. It hurts deep inside, and we try to prevent that because it's a lot like losing a family member or a close friend.

FOURTEEN
Gopher Hunting
"We might not be as lucky the next time"

The Minorcans brought many of their customs with them to the New World. The indentured workers found mostly misery when they docked off the Florida coast. Thick forests and swamps greeted them. Food was scarce, but the Minorcans discovered there were gopher tortoises or turtles in Florida. The gopher turtle was easily trapped and became a steady source of meat.

In those days, the gopher tortoise was plentiful all over Florida, although today, they're a state-designated Threatened Species. The gopher likes sandy high lands where it's easy to dig their burrows and find low-growing plants and grasses since they're herbivorous animals.

Our families followed the Minorcan tradition of hunting gophers, mainly during the summer when the mullet wasn't running on the beach. These days, they call gophers Highland Turtles, but no matter the name, our families loved gopher stew. My father, Pop, and their extended families went gopher hunting for a week at a time. They'd camp all around Silver Springs, the Ocala area, Live Oak, Perry, Dunnellon, and Rainbow Springs—wherever there was good water and wood to burn for our campfires. The young guys loved swimming in the Rainbow River, even though it was cold as hell. Sometimes the older men would go swimming, depending on how much they had to drink.

Gophers love the sandy blackjack oak ridges to dig their holes. Blackjack oaks are small oak trees, and the wood is used mostly for fence posts, railroad ties, and fuel, but they also supply cover and habitat for many birds and animals. Our gopher hunting trips were on some of the hottest days of the year, but the excitement of the hunt and camping out every night was so much fun. Not to mention, the gophers added to our income. We sold most of them to neighbors and townspeople around St. Augustine and the beaches for a dollar apiece, as I recall.

My job was to drag a Croker sack stuffed with the gophers we caught. I was only seven or eight when I began accompanying Pop and the others on these hunting trips. When I was about twelve, I'd go by myself in search of gophers or with one of my friends. We hunted gophers with a wooden pole about 25 feet long and an inch thick. The pole had a steel rod attached to one end with a hook on the end of the rod. The hook was bent and filed off to a flat surface. Usually, we made the hook from a Model A Ford brake rod. We cut an X in the wood to indicate which way the steel hook at the other end was pointed, either up or down.

We jammed the hook end into the hole, and if the gopher was in the burrow, we could feel the hook scraping his shell. At this point, we moved the hook around, trying to slip it under the gopher and catch the bottom of the shell. Then we started pulling him out.

Often, we would catch a gopher out of his hole, eating grass or sunning. As soon as he saw us, it was a race to catch it before the tortoise made it back to its hole. You would be surprised how fast those buggers could run. Occasionally we'd find a female gopher on her back trying to right herself. Pop said that was the way gophers mated. I'm not sure that was the case, but he told me the male would turn the female over with the bull horn under his head. When he finished, he would leave her like that.

Pop said, "That's a hell of a way to treat a lady friend." He'd have me turn her over and put her in the Croker sack.

Pop and I were hunting together on a gopher hunt one day near Silver Springs, and we had five or six gophers in the sack. We discovered a big hole, and Pop said this was a good one, and if we caught another, we'd head back to camp. I was glad to hear that because it was hot as blazes, and those gophers in the sack were getting heavy.

On his knees, Pop kept pushing the pole into the tortoise's burrow until he was down on his belly. About that time, he must have felt something at the other end because he laughed and said, "There you are fellow. I feel you, now if I can just get you hooked you rascal."

He suddenly stiffened and, in a quiet voice, said, "Bubba, stand still. Don't move even a little."

Pop had taught me when hunting or fishing or whatever we were doing that when he said, "Don't move," or "Stop," or "Quiet," you don't ask questions. There's no time to explain things when danger is near. He'd say, "Listen to me the first time and do exactly what I say. And don't ask why at the time. Just do it!"

So, I stopped dead still without a word.

Just as I froze, the granddaddy of all diamondback rattlesnakes slithered slowly out of that hole right over Pop's arm. I was only a couple of feet from Pop, and I could see this big boy's forked tongue sliding in and out of his mouth, tasting the air as he moved past Pop, over the gopher's mound of sand. He paused for a second and then continued off through the grass.

Pop wanted to be sure the rattler was gone and told me not to move until he said so. I'm not sure I could have moved if I wanted to. As I watched it slither away, it seemed like that snake was fifty feet long. Finally, after the rattler was out of sight for at least five minutes, Pop said, "I think he's far enough away. Let's ease out of here."

I thought we should go after the snake and asked Pop, "Are we going to kill him?"

Pop said, "You know, he could have bitten me, or bitten you if he wanted to strike us, but for some reason he didn't. He spared us, so we gonna spare him."

"What about the big gopher in that hole, Poppa? You said you felt him. You going just go off and leave him?"

"Boy you got a lot to learn about life and pushing your luck. That big old rattler may have a wife or a passel of other snakes in that hole and we might not be as lucky the next time. You got me?"

"Yes sir, I got you."

"Besides I need to go to camp and get a good shot of moonshine and check my pants, because I may have messed in them?"

He smiled when he said that, and I asked him if he did mess his pants. "No, I don't think I did, but I came awfully close."

That night around the campfire during supper, the men told tales about rattlesnakes and how they make their homes in gopher holes. After that experience with the rattler that crawled over Pop's arm, I was much more careful in those woods, especially around the gopher holes.

One day when we were hunting gophers, Pop asked me if I knew how the gopher got its name. When I said I didn't, he explained it this way: "A lot of Black people say that God made the turtle, then the devil said he could make one too. But the gopher didn't turn out like the turtle, so the devil said, "Well, it will *go for one.* So, they called it a gopher."

And he laughed.

FIFTEEN

Poisonous Snakes — A Serious Danger in the Woods
"His forked tongue flicking up and down"

The diamondback was as big as my leg, as long as our jeep, coiled and shaking his rattles.

Growing up in the country, walking or riding a bicycle on sandy roads, I always encountered snakes. Eastern diamondback rattlesnakes were common in the scrubland and woods filled with saw palmettos and pine trees. But in North Florida, we'd run across plenty of other poisonous snakes, including the smaller pygmy rattlesnake, the canebrake or timber rattler, and in swampy areas and near most waterways, you'll find the Florida cottonmouth moccasin. The colorful but deadly coral snake can also be found in the area, although I've never bumped into one.

Here's how we came to meet this particular giant rattlesnake. It was a hot summer day in 1952 when I accompanied Louis Weber to Dr. Roberts' house on the inland waterway. Dr. Roberts allowed Louis to stable his horse on his ranch, and we were on our way to feed him.

Louis drove his jeep down a narrow single-lane dirt road when he spotted the huge rattler. How big was it? The diamondback rattler's tail was on one side of the road, and his head was on the other. Louis hit the brakes, and we watched the snake slither slowly toward the thick undergrowth. We couldn't believe the size of the snake.

The thought may have flitted through our teenage brains that no one would believe how big the snake was unless we showed it to them. How else do you explain what we did next? We leaped from the jeep, searching for something to kill him with. I picked up a tree branch and handed it to Louis, telling him to throw the rattler on his back, and use the limb to pin him down.

"I'll look in the jeep and see if I can find something that we can use to kill this big rascal," I said.

I found a large screwdriver in Louis's toolbox and ran back to see the angry snake shaking his rattles like he was playing in a band. His head swayed back and forth, trying to strike at us. I picked up another tree limb and told Louis to hold him down while I pinned his head. It took some doing, but we did it, and I kneeled next to his head. I placed the screwdriver on top of his head and used another piece of wood as a hammer. His head was his big as my fist, and when I drove that screwdriver through his head, his mouth flew open, revealing two vicious inch-long fangs spitting out the deadly venom that can kill animals and humans if left untreated.

We stood on the limbs holding the diamondback down until he stopped moving. After we were sure he was dead, I pulled the screwdriver out of the ground, keeping his head impaled on the screwdriver, and we dragged him over to the jeep. Louis took his tail, and I carted the rest of him, and we laid the body across the vehicle's hood.

We drove to Dr. Roberts's ranch with the giant rattler draped over the hood. Dr. Roberts wasn't home, but Mrs. Roberts and her daughter came out and examined the rattlesnake. Mrs. Roberts said, "Oh, my God that is the biggest one I've ever seen. How did you kill it?"

We told them the story, and Mrs. Roberts was shocked. She told us never to do anything like that again. "A snake as big as that has more than enough venom to kill you before you can get to the hospital. A rattler can strike you before your brain knows to scream."

That scared the hell out of us, and we sat in her kitchen and started shaking, thinking about what we had done and how close we had come to danger, maybe even death.

Louis and I took the snake back to his father's garage, who displayed it there for a couple of days. People came from all over to see it. Mr. Weber then had it skinned and hung on the back wall of his garage. It became quite a conversation piece for his customers.

***

I encountered a rattlesnake while riding my bicycle through the dirt road between my house and 16th Avenue in Jacksonville Beach. The road was extremely sandy, and people got stuck there quite often. On this day, I was riding in one of the sandy ruts, and I had to stand to peddle, using all my weight and strength to keep from falling. I was focused on peddling through that sand, not on the road ahead. Before I knew it, I had ridden up on a rattlesnake laying lengthwise inside the rut, sunning himself. I rolled over his tail, and the snake swung around and sunk his fangs in the front tire where they got stuck. His fangs in the tire probably saved me from being struck, and I leaped off the bicycle, landing in the bushes.

The rattlesnake was still caught in the front tire, working furiously to get his fangs loose. When he did, he immediately raced away into the bushes on the other side of the road.

All I could think of was to get out of there. I righted my bike and peddled away as fast as I could. It didn't take long before my tire was flat, and I had to push my bike the rest of the way home. I leaned it against the house and went in to tell Grandma and Pop what had happened. When I told Pop I was going out to patch my bicycle tire, he said hold on, "I'll go with you cause that could be very dangerous. I knew of a man that got sick from changing a flat automobile tire. He got fever and nausea and started vomiting."

He told me the story about how a rattlesnake had bitten the man's tire and his fangs had broken off in the tire. The man had cut his finger on the broken fang while changing the tire, and the poison infected him. They took the man to a nearby doctor's office, and got him some antivenom serum. The man recovered and was fortunate that he hadn't received more poison, only enough to make him nauseous.

We took the bike tire off, pulled the inner tube out, and sure enough, there were two fang holes in the innertube. Pop cleaned it off with rubbing alcohol and said to let it stand for a day while it dried out, and we'd patch it the next day and put it back on the bike.

***

Here's another chance meeting with a snake that happened when I was cutting sea oats on the beach, up in the sand dunes. As I moved from one clump of sea oats to another, I encountered one of the biggest snakes I had ever seen. It was a brown rat snake. We also called them gopher snakes because they were often found around and in gopher holes where they like to make their homes. That snake must have been eight feet long because he looked as long as my skeeter. One of the guys wanted to kill him, but I said no, he was harmless to us, and we should let him go. The brown snake didn't pay much attention to us. He just rambled off, looking back at us now and then until he was out of sight.

***

Pop and I had an unusual encounter with a black cottonmouth moccasin, another venomous Florida snake. His bite isn't as deadly as the rattler, but it can still make you sick if you don't get to a doctor or hospital fast enough.

Pop and I were going hunting in Palm Valley, and we planned to also get some oysters at Shell Bluff, on the end of what we called the neck or the Guana. Mr. Mickler was a close friend of Pop's, and kind of a caretaker for the timber company that owned the property. Mr. Mickler had keys to the two gates blocking access to the property, and he had given Pop one of the keys with the promise that only Pop would use the key and not give it to anyone else.

It was about ten to fifteen miles from Mickler's Road in Palm Valley to Shell Bluff, and it was all rough country road that trucks used to haul pine timber. The road had deep ruts and a lot of mud and water that day. We had been driving all morning through this rough terrain with only one stop at Booths Island to go to the bathroom and get out a can of sardines and crackers. Pop said we didn't have time to stop and eat.

About an hour later, we were approaching the savanna, about a mile before the camp we called Shell Bluff. The Guana neck was a peninsula surrounded on both sides by salt water, and it always had water in it. The depth of the water depended on how much rain we'd had and if the ocean tide was high or low.

Pop stopped the Model A before driving through the savanna and retrieved a canvas cover for the radiator. He buckled it down to block any water from coming into the engine compartment and flooding the motor. The covered radiator pushed the water out to each side, and if you kept moving, you could drive through four or five feet of water. Pop had been through the savanna many times and knew the water never rose any higher.

He began driving and was moving along steadily through about four feet of water. The canvas cover kept the water from flooding the engine, but it couldn't keep it from flowing through the floorboards. I kept an eye on the water rising in the back when I spotted a black moccasin on the floorboard. I yelled at Pop to alert him.

"Leave him alone," he said, "I can't stop now because the water would cover the motor but get Betsy out from between the seats. If he starts to move up front between the seats you going to have to shoot him. But for God's sake don't hit the rear tires or we'll be dead in the water."

I grabbed the shotgun and aimed it toward the back seat. The snake was too busy trying to find a way out and return to the savanna to pay attention to me. But when he flipped around toward the front, I thought, *Oh, oh. This is it!*

Before I could point Old Betsy at the intruder, a wave of water flooded in, propelled the moccasin to the side of the running board and washed the snake right out of our skeeter.

"Pop, Pop," I yelled. "He gone out through the running board."

I could see Pop was relieved. "That damn son a bitch almost got us in serious trouble," he said. "Keep watching in case he comes back in. We only got about five more minutes and we will be through the savanna."

The water had risen over our feet, but now it began going down. We drove the rest of the way along the edge of the savanna, and it was muddy, but the water was only about two feet deep. We reached the fork in the road—one went to the left to the Guana Neck, where the Guana River and Intracoastal Waterway came together, and the other to the right out of the savanna and into very high palmetto bushes. The palmettos were so high they'd grown over the road, making it seem more like an animal trail. Pop put the skeeter in low gear and slowly plowed through the bushes for nearly a half hour before we broke into the clearing on the Intracoastal Waterway.

We had arrived at Shell Bluff.

Looking back on all we had to go through to get to Shell Bluff, I see now that Pop considered it a challenge to travel through the worse terrain, all the way there and back, to get some oysters. It was almost like a game to him. Of course, he'd have a great story to tell when we returned home because he'd accomplished something most people would not even try. And the big moccasin I watched wash in and out of the Model A only added to the story. Pop was the only one in his family that would tackle such a challenge, and he loved it!

***

I'll leave you with one last snake story. My father built my sister and me a

10' x 10' wooden playhouse when I was five and Joyce was ten. The playhouse sat on concrete blocks positioned at each corner to keep the structure off the ground. I asked my father to include a trap door in the floor as an escape hatch from imaginary bad guys or Indians or whatever game I was playing. I decided to dig a channel in the ground beneath the cabin leading from the trap door to the back of the playhouse to make it easier to escape my make-believe enemies.

The digging wasn't easy since there wasn't much space to move under the playhouse. But I was single-minded, even at that young age. I lay on my side, scooping out dirt, pushing it aside, and making steady progress. As I dug, my head was about six inches from one of the corner concrete blocks.

My mind was already working through the various adventures I'd have in the playhouse, using the trap door and escape tunnel to outwit pirates and other villains. Suddenly, I heard rattling coming from the blocks near my head. Looking for the source of the strange noise, I saw a rattlesnake staring back at me. He was sliding out of one of the holes in the concrete blocks but stopped when he saw me. I stared in horror at his forked tongue flicking up and down. The snake's milky blue eyes were locked on mine.

Holding my breath, I slowly backed away and scrambled up through the trap door just as the rattler slid out of the hole in the block. But I didn't hang around and hightailed it out of the playhouse. That thing scared me to death. When I told my father about it, he said the snake didn't strike me because he probably could not coil. He said I was a lucky little boy. They searched for the snake, but it was gone. After that incident, my father covered up my trap door and said, "No more trap door. Got me!"

I was in total agreement. No more trap door. Not on my life. That was my first introduction to a rattlesnake, but as you've already read, there were more to come.

PART THREE

High School Days

Bobby's Rules to Live by:

6. Don't audit your life. Show up and make the most of it now.

7. We must learn to forgive because if not we are the only one we hurt the most.

8. The most important sex organ is your brain.

ONE

A Skeeter of My Own
Built from scratch and old parts. Fantastic!

I built my first car from a rusted-out Model A Ford, but before I tell you about that, you need to know about my first bicycle. Grandma and Pop gave me a nice used bike for Christmas when I was twelve. Owning a bike meant I didn't have to walk from where we lived in Adamsville to the 16th Avenue and 3rd Street school bus stop and back home every day. The roads I biked were unpaved, consisting of what Pop called "white sugar sand," which made peddling extremely hard. And when it rained, those dirt roads were a mess. Even cars got stuck in the mud. But I loved that bike, and the daily peddling developed strong leg muscles that helped me when I began playing basketball.

I still had that bike when I started talking to H. L., my good buddy down the road, about his brother's old Model A. The car was in terrible shape and an eyesore in the neighborhood. It had been sitting up on blocks for four or five years. H. L. said it was sitting in their yard because it would cost too much to get it hauled off.

Anyone could see the car wasn't worth a penny in its present state. All four tires were dry rotted and flat. The body was barely hanging on the frame, and all the windows, including the windshield, were busted out. No headlights or taillights, either. It looked like someone had taken out their anger on it with a sledgehammer. If you looked up "Junk Car" in the dictionary, you'd probably see a picture of that Model A.

Despite the condition of that junker, I thought I could do something with it and offered his brother my bicycle in exchange. Of course, he didn't hesitate and agreed to the trade. Man, was I excited!

I hurried home to tell Pop about my deal, but he didn't share my excitement. "Don't tell me you traded your bike for that old piece of junk sitting over there in the Dorty's yard?" he said.

When I confirmed that it was the same piece of junk I now owned, he said, "Well you're going to have quite a time getting that thing to run."

All I could think about was having a beach buggy of my own. I could barely contain my excitement and replied, "I can do it Pop, with your help."

"Oh, no," he said. "I didn't make that deal. But I'll show you what to do and you're going to do it all on your own. You made the deal so you're going to have to follow through with it."

That was fine with me because I knew Pop could fix anything, and if he showed me how, I could do it, too. "Thanks, Pop," I said. "The first thing we have to do is go over there and pull it home."

Pop said, "Dammit! I'm already in it whether I want to or not. I ought to box your ears for trading your bike for that mess. How you going to pull it home when it got no tires on it?"

I had an answer for that. "We can take the tires and wheels off number six. They just need a little air."

Pop seemed impressed that I had come up with a solution. "Okay boy, that's your first start. Go out there and block up number six and get those tires off and put them in the back of my truck."

I did it, and after supper, we went to H. L.'s house to haul my "new" car home. When Pop got a good look at that wreck, he thought I had lost my mind. I'm sure he believed I'd never get that thing running. After a couple of weeks of working on it, so did I.

Before I continue with this tale, let me explain what I meant by the number six. This Model A wasn't the first junker we'd brought home. A lot of people had old broken-down automobiles sitting around in those days. They couldn't afford to have them towed to the junkyard, and Pop would offer to take them away. He'd put tires on them and pull them to the house. At the house, he parked them out in the Palmetto Patch. That's what we called the acreage around our house. It was wide-open, and nobody lived within a mile or so. Pop would paint a number on each one, and when he wanted a part, he'd either get it himself or tell me to get it off number three or four. He'd use the part to fix his skeeter or whatever he was working on. He used those parts to repair our cars and our neighbors. He'd often repair their vehicles for nothing or charge them only a little to bring in some money for the family.

After we hauled the old junker home, Pop helped me strip it down to the frame. He instructed me to sand down the frame to get as much rust off as possible. That was a lot of work, but I did it. He told me, "Buy yourself a can of rust-proofing red paint and paint that frame."

So that's what I did. I bought cans of Rust-Oleum and painted the entire frame from the rear end differential to the steering column. Pop replaced the old cowling on the engine, the gas tank, and the windshield. Next, we built a wooden body on the frame and put the bucket seats back in it. The buggy had no doors, but we cut out the driver and passenger sides so you could climb in and out. The finished product looked something like a bumper car from the side. A four-by-eight piece of Masonite served as the roof for my skeeter.

My grandmother covered the bucket seats with white cloth patterned with red roses and green leaves. Those seats stood out like a sore thumb, and everybody got a laugh out of it. She also made a padded cushion for the back wooden seat. Now my skeeter was taking shape.

We worked on the hood for some time to be sure the engine cowling and the hood matched up with the radiator. Then we bought some headlights and attached them to the frame because we didn't have any fenders. The frame stuck out about a foot and a half in front of the radiator. The taillights were attached to the wooden body in the back, and I added three spare tire racks: one on each side and one in the back.

I painted the skeeter black so you couldn't see it at night on the beach. It took a couple of coats because the wood soaked up the paint. I painted the Masonite roof and the 2" x 2" corner posts holding up the roof. It also supported the fold-up hood, and the radiator supported the other end of the hood. The entire process took months of hard work, but I loved the challenge and never gave up on that old junker. Owning a beach buggy not only gave me a sense of pride but opened the door to personal freedom and many more adventures, as you'll soon see.

Beach buggies, aka skeeters, like this one roamed the beaches of Jacksonville and St. Augustine in the mid-1940s. Photo courtesy of the St. Augustine Record.

TWO
Adventures in the Beach Graveyard
"I guess these belong to you"

The distance from Jacksonville Beach to St. Augustine or Vilano Beach is about thirty miles. When I was young, it was thirty miles of open sandy shore and bad patches of wet coquina with deep ruts where beach buggies drove on high and medium-high tides. It was and still is very treacherous in some places. Of course, you can't drive on most of the beach anymore.

The worst place was the Graveyard, about a ten-mile stretch south of Mickler's Pier to the first well. The Graveyard has swallowed many vehicles, primarily those driven by people unfamiliar with the beach and where and how to drive on it. Sometimes they went too close to the water and hit a washout or a slough run-out. Inevitably, ninety percent of them would either stop or slow down.

Big mistake.

When you hit a water spot like that, you need to speed up as fast as possible and steer the vehicle toward the dunes with your foot down hard on the gas. The sand and water are unforgiving, and they want your car. You handle a coquina patch the same way. There is usually no hard bottom, and the vehicle will sink in a few seconds if you don't give it the gas and get through that spot. The coquina patch might only be ten to thirty feet, and you need to move through it quickly.

It was about midnight when my buddy H. L. and I were hunting for turtle eggs. I was driving my beach buggy, and the tide was about halfway in when we spotted a car with its parking lights on down near the water. We had saved the vehicles of people stuck on the beach many times, and I felt this would be another time. This was confirmed when we saw a man and lady waving frantically at us. The lady had her hands in a praying position begging us to stop.

Of course, I stopped and asked, "What can we do for you folks," although I could see their car was in trouble.

The man was breathing hard. His eyes were wide. He said, "For God's sake, we need to get my car unstuck and off this beach. That's a new Buick Skylark and I just got it three months ago. If you can help us, believe me, I will never come on the beach with my car again."

The tide was coming in fast, and small waves were starting to lap at the wheels of the man's new Buick. He was desperate. Tears were streaming down his face. "Please," he pleaded, "you have to help us."

He and his lady friend were panicking, and I didn't blame them since they were about to lose their car to the high tide. I tried to calm them but explained, "The problem is the closest wrecker is in St. Augustine, and if we find one, it's going to cost you two to three hundred dollars for them to come all way down here in the middle of the night. And when they get here, if their tow cable isn't long enough to reach you, there's very little they can do. They're not going to put their wrecker down on this beach to get stuck like your car."

The young man broke in and said, "I don't care what it costs, I got to get it off the beach."

I said, "The other problem we got is that the tide is coming in fast and in less than an hour, those waves will be washing against the car. I hate to ask, but do you have insurance on it?"

He said he did, but that didn't help his situation. "Mister, are you telling me there's no way I can get my car out before the tide comes in and covers it?"

"I'm only trying to prepare you for the worst," I said. "But hold on and let me and my friend take a closer look."

I drove my beach buggy down to his car, put on the high beams, and shined the spotlight on the Buick. The front end was sitting in about six inches of water, and the front tires had settled into the wet sand. It wasn't what I'd call suction-type wet sand, but the sand was wet enough that the tires would continue sinking as the waves inched closer.

The Buick was a heavy car. Not a good sign at all. I turned and asked him how he got in this fix.

He said, "I stopped up there on the highway by that little round water well, and we walked down the road to the beach. The sand near the water seemed real hard and I thought we would just come down and go for a ride on the beach in my new car. I drove right down the sandy road from the well with no problem. When I came over the second little dune onto the beach, I swung down to turn around and hit a wash out. I stopped as soon as I could and tried to back up, but my rear wheels just started spinning and digging in the sand. Soon it wouldn't move at all, backwards or frontwards. And that's what happened, mister."

When he called me *mister*, I interrupted him, told him to call me Bobby, and introduced my friend H. L. He said, "Okay, Bobby, if you get me out with your buggy, I will pay you $200."

I told him I had some experience at this, but "I get concerned every time I pull somebody out that I'm going to break something in my buggy and that bothers me. But you just hold on for a minute."

I asked H. L. to get our shovel, and we walked to the front of the car. "It looks like the sand has a little more bottom to it going forward," I said to H. L. after examining the front wheels. "I think we can dig out in front and back of each tire, where the sand has banked up. If we do the same to the back tires where they have some room and level ground to move back and forth, I just might be able to drive the bitch out. What do you think?"

"Bobby, I've seen you drive out cars in worse shape than this," my friend said. "But once you get it moving, you better not stop till you get up on that hard road. That means you got to go forward fast, spin around and come back fast to start over the first high water dunes. You know as well as me if you stopped that heavy car anywhere down here it's going to sink in the sand a couple of inches and will be hard to get moving again."

I agreed because H. L. wasn't telling me anything I didn't know. "Let's go talk to the car owner," I said.

I told the Buick's owner it was too dangerous to put the beach buggy down there because the wheels would spin when we started pulling his car and break through that crust, and we'd be stuck too. "Then we all would be in a hell of a mess."

Here's what else I said to him: "Sir, I was born and raised on this beach. Driving on it is a real professional job, and you must know what you're doing. I have driven a lot of cars out of the sand and saved the vehicles. If you want me to try, I think I can drive your car out and put it over the dunes and onto the road. But I don't want you to blame me if anything happens because once I get it out and moving, I can't stop until I get it up and over the sand dunes to the road. You understand that part?"

He nodded, and I continued talking.

"And I will have to go down the beach fast, make a quick turn around and come back at about fifty or sixty miles an hour to go up over the tidal dune on to the sandy road that goes up through the big dunes and up to the paved road."

It seemed the man was following me, so I added, "My buddy here will park the dune buggy, so the lights are shining on the spot I will need to go over the first tide dunes. That will be the spot where the sandy road comes down through the big dunes you came down on. You guys will then ride with H. L. in our buggy up over the dunes, where hopefully me and your car will be waiting for you."

He seemed to consider this before saying, "Well, Mr. Bobby, I don't have a hell of a lot to lose, do I? If I don't do anything, I lose my car. But if you think you can get back over the dunes to the road, then let's do it." He reached over, shook my hand, and said, "It's a deal. Go for it!"

H. L. and I began digging out the wheels. After we finished digging, I opened the driver's door to get in, and a pair of women's panties fell out. I picked them up and examined the lacy undergarment for a moment before handing them to the lady. "I guess these belong to you," I said with a big smile.

She returned my smile and said, "So that's where they were. I thought I had lost them." We all laughed as she took the panties and stuffed them into her purse.

Still thinking about the young lady's panties, I climbed into the Skylark, started her up, and put her into gear. I eased forward a little, then back several times until I felt the tires hit new sand. I gave her the gas at that point but without spinning the wheels until I felt the car come up on the crust, and then I gave it more gas until the Buick was up and running fast, about 35 miles an hour. My buggy's spotlight illuminated the track, and I spun her around without stopping and headed toward the lights of my beach buggy.

I hit the sandy road over the first dune doing fifty miles an hour. The front tires left the ground a little as we went over the dune and came down. Other beach buggies had left their mark, and I aimed for the ruts carved into the dune. Driving uphill through soft white sand naturally slowed me down. Even though the speedometer was reading forty miles an hour, the car only plugged along at about twenty miles an hour since the back wheels were spinning at high speed.

Plowing ahead, I was about three-quarters of the way to the paved road and the artesian well. I mashed the gas pedal to the floor and kept driving until I pulled out onto State Road A1A. I think I was just as excited as I knew the car's owner and his girlfriend would be.

In just a few minutes, I saw the lights of my beach buggy as H. L. ferried the Buick's owner and his girlfriend, who'd lost her panties, to our rendezvous spot. The man leaped from the buggy, whooping like he'd won some great prize, and hugged my neck. "I got forty dollars cash in my wallet," he told me. "But I can write you a check for the rest of the two hundred dollars I promised you."

That was very nice of him, but I said, "We'll take the forty dollars and call it even. No problem." But I advised him to be more careful the next time he went for a ride on the beach.

Shaking his head, he said, "That will be a cold day in hell before I ever ride on the beach in my car again. You can take that to the bank."

H. L. and I said our goodbyes, jumped in the buggy, and motored down the beach to continue our turtle egg hunt, waving to the happy couple as we left. I'm sure he learned that driving in soft sand anywhere is tricky, even if your vehicle is specially equipped. Although I suspect he had other things on his mind that night.

THREE
Cutting Sea Oats
"My legs refused to move"

During the summer of 1950, '51, and '52, we cut sea oats for my buddy Jim McGann's father, who owned a flower shop. The flower shop was in Jackson-ville Beach, although the family lived in Ponte Vedra Beach, where we brought the plants. Jim's dad had a barn behind his house where he'd dry the sea oats on racks until they turned a beautiful golden brown. Mr. McGann used them in flower arrangements and sold them to other florists across the USA.

I was the only one with a beach buggy and knew how to drive in the sand dunes with a trailer to haul out our cut sea oats, which grew wild on the dunes. Mr. McGann paid for the gas for my skeeter, plus paid the other boys and me for each bundle we cut. We did all the work, and he reaped the rewards of our labor.

Our crew of cutters included me, Jim McGann, Robert Taylor, Bill Broome, Nat Frazer, Joe Conan, and a few others from time to time. We were a rough and rowdy bunch of beach boys.

Each one of us had a razor-sharp machete. We would hold the sea oat stem in one hand, or more than one stem if they were growing close together, and with a single swipe, you heard a *Ping*, the sound of the machete cutting through the thin stem. When we were all cutting, you could hear pinging everywhere. After cutting twenty-five plants, we stopped, took out one of the twisters Mr. McGann had supplied and tied the stems into a bundle. We'd drop the bundle to the ground and keep cutting and wrapping. Each of us had a different color twister to identify our bundles since we were paid by the bundle. Mr. McGann only gave us ten cents a bundle, but it added up. And remember, this was about seventy years ago, and you could buy a lot more in those days since a 1950 dollar is worth about ten dollars today.

We cut sea oats from St Augustine's Matanzas Inlet north to the jetties at the St Johns River north of Atlantic Beach. That's a long way, between sixty and seventy-five miles of beach and dunes. We knew we were in for a long day's work and brought lunch and water to drink or went hungry since we were miles from civilization most of the time.

Nat sliced his hand on his machete on one of these outings. We had a first aid kit with us, but this was a bad cut, and it wouldn't stop bleeding. One of the guys tied a tourniquet around his forearm, but it kept bleeding. That's when the fussing and fighting began about who would take him to the doctor. Poor Nat was bleeding like a stuck pig, but none of us wanted to stop cutting. Finally, I'd had enough of the bickering and said, "It's my skeeter, and I'm going to take Nat to the doctor, but you boys are on your own because I'm not coming back for anyone."

They all bitched and moaned for a few minutes, but no one wanted to hoof it back some twenty miles. We loaded our sea oats into the trailer, and I drove to Jacksonville Beach, where I dropped off the other boys. I took Nat to Dr. Roberts' office to get him patched up. You'd think Nat would be grateful, but he was pissed and couldn't get over the fact none of us wanted to stop cutting sea oats while he was bleeding to death—or so he kept telling us. And not just for a few days or weeks, but kept after us for several years.

Many issues arose with our group of sea oat cutters, boys of thirteen to sixteen years old, out there on our own. In those days cutting sea oats was perfectly legal, except in state parks or private property. This was before the government passed laws all up and down the southeastern Atlantic coast protecting sea oats. Here in Florida, a statute states it's unlawful "to cut, harvest, remove, or eradicate any of the grass commonly known as sea oats." If caught, you're looking at a year in jail and a fine of up to $1,000. The statute is on the books because sea oats, with their deep root systems, protect the sand dunes. Of course, we knew nothing of that growing up.

One day, long before that law was passed, we were cutting sea oats on Little Talbot Island. We had never cut on Big Talbot Island, which was on the other side of the Nassau Sound separating the two islands. That day the sea oats were in short supply on Little Talbot Island, and we decided to pack up and head across Nassau Sound to the larger island.

Jimmy McGann and I planned to swim across with our machetes and twisters and start cutting oats while the other guys drove around to the Big Talbot Bridge. It would take them at least thirty minutes to get there with my skeeter and trailer, and we could have a lot of sea oats cut by then.

It seemed like a good plan at the time, but I'd quickly learn it was a bad idea.

Jimmy and I used the twisters to tie our sneakers to our belts. Gripping our machetes, we dove in and began swimming toward Big Talbot. Jimmy was one of the stars on our high school swim team and had won medals at various swim meets. He soon left me in his wake, pulling away by twenty-five to thirty yards. I hadn't counted on the current being so strong, and as hard as I tried, it was a struggle to make any progress. I dropped the machete, but that wasn't much help. So next, I unbuckled my belt and slipped out of my pants, which floated away along with my sneakers.

I kept slapping and kicking at the water, but ten minutes later, I was so exhausted I was floating face down, thinking my time on this earth was about up. Images and thoughts of past experiences drifted in and out of my mind before everything went blank. My brain must have shut down in preparation for my demise.

Before that happened, something hit me in the head, and through my exhaustion, I heard Jimmy yelling, "Get up you damn fool. Are you going to drown in three feet of water?"

He pulled me up, and my feet touched the sandy bottom. My legs refused to move, and Jimmy dragged me to shore. I flopped down on the sand like one of those mullet Pop and I caught, but without the strength to lift my head. I lay there for about fifteen minutes until life returned to my arms and legs.

When I finally rolled over, there was Jimmy, and I felt more than a little foolish. He was sitting there grinning like a possum eating a sweet potato. Shaking his head, he said, "Solano, you owe me one."

Truer words were never spoken. "That's for damn sure, Jimmy," I agreed. The rest of our gang pulled up in a little while, and Jimmy couldn't wait to tell them how he saved me from drowning while I floated in three feet of water. Everyone laughed, and I must have been a funny sight lying there in my underwear with my pants, sneakers, and machete at the bottom of the Sound, but I joined in the laughter. After drinking some water, they started cutting sea oats. But not me. I collapsed on the beach and slept for at least an hour.

***

Little Talbot and Big Talbot Islands were National Parks covered with sea oats. Since it was illegal to cut sea oats in National Parks, we would cut them at night when the moon was full. We'd go to Mayport, take the last ferry over the St. Johns River to Fort George Island and hang out until dark when the gates closed at the park. Then with the buggy's lights off, we would sneak into the park by driving over the dunes or around the locked gates.

We did this for a few weeks until the park people added a night guard who stopped us on the main road before we could sneak into the park. The guard was a good old boy, who came up to me on the driver's side. He looked at the buggy filled with rough-looking teens and the trailer we were hauling, then said, "Boys, somebody's been cutting sea oats on the islands. You know they are National Parks and cutting sea oats is against the law."

We all managed to look surprised and innocent as the guard continued his speech. "We have traced their tracks, and they'll have to pay a $500 fine and maybe spend a few nights in jail. Now, I don't know where you guys are headed but if you see them, give them this warning for me. I'd hate to put them in jail over a few sea oats. Okay? You guys be careful going home, but you better not come this way again. We might get the wrong idea."

That was the end of cutting sea oats on the Talbot Islands.

FOUR

Invading the "Rich Folks" Pool on Ponte Vedra Beach
"We made a mad dash for the buggy"

Late one night H. L. and I were driving south toward St. Augustine and stopped at the set of poles blocking vehicles from continuing up the beach. I knew the barrier marked the border between Duval County and St. Johns Counties. There was a Coast Guard tower there at the time. Another set of poles at the far end of Ponte Vedra Beach prevented cars from coming from the south. That set of poles was located right at the Oasis Bar, or Barney's as everyone called it. Ponte Vedra Beach was between the two groups of poles, and Tola had told me the poles were put there by the "Ponte Vedra rich folks" who didn't want anyone driving on their beach.

Those poles didn't stop us for long. I went up on the dunes and around the first poles and headed south. It was a warm summer night, and as we passed the exclusive Ponte Vedra Inn, H. L. said, "Hey, let's sneak a swim in the club's pool and cool off."

It was about midnight, and not a soul was in sight, so I agreed but said, "We have to be very quiet, or they'll catch us."

I parked next to the sea wall in front of the beach club and cut off the engine. All was quiet, and we climbed out of the buggy and scrambled over the wall. H. L. headed for the diving board while I started down the steps into the pool rather than diving, trying not to make any noise.

At the top of the high dive, H. L. bounced up and down, preparing to make his first dive. Before he did, I screamed, "No! There's no water in the pool."

It was pitch black as I'd stepped into the pool and couldn't see the bottom, but I didn't need the light to see there was no water. H. L. almost fell off the board when he heard me yell and came flying down the ladder.

I'm scrambling up the pool steps when all the lights come on. Oh, hell, I'm thinking, the night guards heard us.

We made a mad dash for the buggy, and as we pulled away, the guard screamed, "We are going to get you guys and put you in jail."

Well, they'd have to catch us first. I floored the skeeter, and we left the guards and the Ponte Vedra Inn far behind. When we approached the second set of poles near Barney's, we saw flashing red lights, and I said, "Damn, they must have called the police."

The cops were standing next to their police car on the road, looking down at us. I cut off our taillights so they couldn't read our license plates and steered the buggy over the dunes and around the poles. Stomping the gas, we flew across the hard-packed sand and left Barney's and the police behind.

We never heard anything more about that issue.

FIVE
Good Times at Fletcher High School
"They were always great times"

Good times come and go, but I consider my senior year in high school as one of the best years—if not the best—of my life. If you could find Fletcher students who were 10th, 11th, and 12th grades in 1954, I'm sure they'd agree that was one of the greatest years of their lives.

What made that year so much fun? It's hard to pick out any single activity because we enjoyed what seemed like a series of nonstop parties and dances. The school sponsored dances on Friday nights after football, basketball games, and other sporting events. Those were fun, but the best times were when all our friends came together for parties up and down the coast, including at Dr. Roberts's hunting cabin in Palm Valley and the Dickinson's cabin on the inland waterway. We threw huge beach parties at the jetties in Atlantic Beach and the Mickler's Pier on A1A in Palm Valley.

Another highlight was caravanning to the Surfside Casino in Vilano Beach. Louis Weber packed his jeep with kids, and we loaded Bill Hires' and my beach buggy with guys and girls. We'd drive on the beach from Jacksonville Beach to the Surfside Casino in Vilano Beach.

Bill Broome (his nickname was Brush) in his dad's Kaiser sedan would lead the rest of the folks in their cars down State Road A1A. But first, we all gathered at Bill's Drive-In before making the trip to the Surfside Casino, where we would dance and party until midnight. I loved to dance, and would you believe there's a full-page picture of Barbara Tucker and me in the Fletcher High year-book? We'd been voted Best Dancers by the student body.

The Surfside Casino wasn't a gambling hall but a popular entertainment center featuring local bands. Our most potent drinks were beer, and that was all we needed to dance and enjoy the time with our friends. These parties took place on Friday and Saturday nights; they were always great times.

The rides on the beach were so popular we had to draw names to see who would ride with us since we only had three vehicles capable of driving over the sand. That limited it to about fifteen or sixteen people taking the beach ride, and there were usually many more kids ready to party.

It's hard to believe so many teenagers partied together over multiple week-ends. We got along great together for the most part, except for the usual bicker-ing about girlfriends and boyfriends. And like the good times, these friends are still a part of my feel-good memories: Mayo Gabriel, Claude Midgett, James Minton, David Gard, Franklin Dickinson, Louis Weber, and Jeff Roberts. There were others, but these guys stood out because they were always ready to go. We all had our girlfriends, and sometimes we'd swap around, but it was always in good fun. And when you put young men and women together, you know there's going to be a lot of what we called "smooching" on the beach, in the cars, and on the dance floor.

We had some wonderful times at the Surfside Casino, but sadly, the county tore down the aging building in the 1970s and converted the site to an ocean-front park with restrooms and parking. The Solano family currently owns the Surfside Cottages adjoining the parking lot, and we've been renovating them.

Our 1954 class seemed to attract a lot of kids from the 10th and 11th grades who were eager to party with us. All of them knew about my low-income situation but never mentioned it, and I never let it bother me. During lunch, sometimes, my classmates would come over to see what Bobby was eating because, thanks to my grandmother, my lunch bag always contained something exotic to my more civilized schoolmates. I might have fried mullet and coleslaw, fried squirrel, rabbit, chicken, quail, pork, or venison sandwiches on any given day. I thought I was the luckiest guy in the school lunchroom, which was great fun for them and me.

But I couldn't escape the facts of life. One incident stands out in my memory, reminding me how the Solano family was different from those of the other kids I knew. After school each day, the yellow bus dropped us off at the corner of 16th Avenue and 3rd Street, near a little grocery store. With the exuberance of middle schoolers released from classes, we would jostle one another and joke around.

Scrambling off the bus, most kids raced to the grocery store to buy a soft drink, ice cream, or a candy bar. As they headed to the store on this day, a couple of my friends called for me to join them. I wanted to go but said, "Sorry, I don't have time. I gotta get home and help Pop work on his car."

The truth was I didn't have a nickel or dime to buy anything. The other kids received lunch money and allowances. I packed my lunch and went home with empty pockets. And that was usually fine with me, but I remember walking away from my friends that day with tears in my eyes. The knowledge of my financial limitations hit home, and as I trudged off toward Adamsville, I made a promise to myself:

When I grow up, there will never be a day when I won't have a dime in my pocket to buy a Pepsi Cola with my friends.

That childhood memory stuck with me for the rest of my life. It was a promise I made to myself that I've never forgotten.

SIX

Firecracker Fun

"That was a close one, guys"

It's the 4th of July 1954. We had just rounded the curve on Atlantic Boulevard by the old Atlantic Beach Hotel. Five of us were crammed in my skeeter, throwing cherry bombs and firecrackers along the road and into the front yards of some of our friend's houses. We weren't bad kids, just a bunch of guys trying to create a bit of action to celebrate our national holiday.

Eddie Cherry—yes, Eddie's last name was Cherry—was in the backseat with Brush Broome and Jeff Roberts, three wild and crazy guys. Joining me up front was my pal H. L. Dorty. Jeff and Eddie were having a blast lighting and throwing the cherry bombs. Before the Child Safety Act of 1966, cherry bombs were packed with a lot more powder and made a terrific explosion when they blew up. We'd yell and whoop with every detonation.

Just as we were going around that corner, here comes old Jarboe passing us on the same curve in the other direction. Jarboe was the Atlantic Beach police constable and considered himself a real cowboy. He wore a big Stetson, carried a pearl-handled revolver, and loved to smoke cigars. Talk about timing being everything—Eddie had just flipped another cherry bomb onto the road, and it went off under Jarboe's police car after he passed us.

We heard the muffler clatter and all kinds of clanging noise rumbled from the underside of his vehicle. The explosion rattled us as much as the police car's tailpipes, and we knew we were in serious trouble if he caught us. I immediately cut off the skeeter's lights and turned left down a side road. I had the pedal to the floor, and everyone held on as I made a series of turns before pulling into Kaye Minchew's yard. Kaye and I were dating, and I was familiar with her yard from having parked there more than a few times. I drove the skeeter behind a thick stand of bamboo canes and turned her off.

"You guys shut up and don't move a muscle," I said. We all hunkered down, waiting to see if the constable had followed us. Sure enough, in about five minutes, Jarboe creeps by with his spotlight scanning both sides of the road. He went by Kaye's house so slowly we could hear the patrol car's tailpipe dragging against the pavement. Everyone froze, watching and waiting for at least five minutes after he disappeared.

I cranked up the skeeter, and we motored toward the Atlantic Beach golf course and slipped out to Atlantic Boulevard, Penman Road, and back to Jacksonville Beach.

"That was a close one, guys," I said. "But we got away clean." I dropped them off at Bill's Drive-In and went home, hoping I'd put that firecracker adventure in my rear-view mirror.

I was in first-period class on Monday morning when the teacher called me up to the front of the room. He handed me a slip of paper that said Coach Brant, the assistant principal, wanted to see me in his office immediately. I didn't think he wanted to congratulate me on my good grades, so I had a bad feeling about being summoned after what happened over the weekend. When I walked into Coach Brant's office, the bad feeling was sitting there wearing a constable's uniform.

Coach Brant was a big guy with a folksy manner and a mane of silver hair. He said, "Solano, the constable here says there's a cutdown skeeter parked outside in the student parking area that looks exactly like the one some boys were riding in and throwing firecrackers in Atlantic Beach Saturday night. They threw one right under his police car and took off and got away. We all know fireworks are illegal in the city limits, don't we?"

I said, "Yes sir, we sure do."

The lawman was staring a hole right through me.

Coach Brant continued, "Constable Jarboe would like to know where you were on Saturday night."

"Well, sir, most of the night, I was at Bill's Drive-In with the rest of the school kids. Then, some of the guys rode down the beach with me before we all went home."

The constable sat there wearing his Stetson and shiny revolver on his hip, giving me the eye before asking, "Were you in Atlantic Beach Saturday night?"

"Oh, no sir, you can check with the rest of the kids that were hanging out at Bill's. I'm sure they'll tell you we were there most of the night."

I felt I had sold it pretty well, but Constable Jarboe wasn't buying it. He said, "Solano, there's only one beach skeeter in Neptune Beach, Atlantic Beach, or Jacksonville Beach that looks like yours. I don't have any proof that it was you, but I'm warning you if I catch you in Atlantic Beach speeding, making noise, or creating any problems I'm going to put you under the jail. You understand?"

"Yes sir, I understand perfectly."

Coach Brandt dismissed me, saying, "Okay, Solano, get outta here while you're ahead of the game and get back to your room."

I was out of there in a flash.

That evening Coach Brant came by to gas up at Weber's Service Station, where I worked from 6:00 to 10:00 almost every night and on weekends. Louis Weber was one of my closest friends, and his father, Mr. Dick Weber, owned the service station and garage.

As I was filling up Mr. Brant's car, he said, "Solano, you better not go to Atlantic Beach if you know what's good for you. Constable Jarboe was upset about that cherry bomb going off under his police car. He said it blew off his muffler and tailpipe. He also said he knew it was your beach buggy and recognized some other gang members from Fletcher. But said he can't prove it."

I listened politely and kept pumping gas.

Ish Brant was a good guy and as smart a country boy as you'd ever meet. At the University of Florida, he'd lettered in track, baseball, and football. At Fletcher, he served as assistant principal, athletic director, and head football coach. Coach Brant later served three terms as Mayor of Neptune Beach and the City Manager of Jacksonville Beach. He was also the last elected Duval County school superintendent.

He ended our gas pump conversation with a warning. "Remember, he'll be looking for that beach buggy of yours if it ever comes to Atlantic Beach."

I can't swear I never went to Atlantic Beach again, but that marked the end of the cherry bomb incident.

SEVEN
Big Cat Scare
"The wail echoed through the woods"

It's late on a Friday night. My team had won another basketball game earlier that night, and instead of joining my teammates to celebrate, I decided to go hunting. I hopped in the beach buggy and headed to Shell Bluff on Booth Island. By midnight I'd churned through the first hammock when my headlights caught the outline of an animal in my path. Its eyes glowed red in the reflected light, staring directly at me. Before I could stomp the brakes, the animal disappeared into the bushes. I didn't know what to think but realized I had seen my first Florida panther. And it was a big one.

I waited a minute while my heart slowed before continuing to my destination, where I hoped to bag some squirrels for Grandma's dinner table. You might ask why I was alone on Booth Island in the middle of the night. Good question, and the answer was I didn't need a reason to go hunting alone. I'd learned from Pop how to be self-sufficient and survive on the beach and in the woods. And after what had been an intense basketball game, I needed time to decompress.

I decided to camp at the old sawmill, where logs were trimmed and cut for the local timber company to haul to its mills. I parked next to a giant pile of sawdust probably forty feet high and built a fire from the scraps of wood scattered around. It didn't take long before I had a nice blaze going. I heated a can of Campbell's Soup and settled down next to the fire, wrapped in a blanket.

The familiar night sounds had faded away when I drove up, but now a chorus of chirping insects and croaking frogs resumed—all of it music to this beach boy's ears. With the heat of the fire warming my body and the soup warming my stomach, I soon drifted off to sleep. But not for long. A shrill, high-pitched scream pierced the night, and I was instantly awake. The wail echoed through the woods, sounding like a woman screaming or moaning in agony.

People always say that the hair on the back of their neck stands up when they're scared. It's true. I was petrified and immediately began tossing more fuel on the fire until the rising flames illuminated my little campsite. That brought some comfort, but I needed more and retrieved my shotgun and rifle from the skeeter. Outside the ring of firelight was total darkness. The sound of that animal scream still rattled in my head, and spending the night in the open didn't seem wise. I grabbed my blankets and crawled into the backseat of the beach buggy with my two weapons.

I lay there quietly for most of the night, staring into the shadows and listening for another bloodcurdling scream that never came. At dawn, I unfolded myself from the back seat of the buggy, built up the fire again, and warmed myself against the morning chill.

After a cup of coffee, I slowly came back to life, and my curiosity won over my fear of whatever creature had shattered my night's sleep. I circled the area in the morning light, searching for tracks or other signs I'd been visited during the night. Not far away was the mountain of sawdust looming over everything.

As I glanced around, I told myself, "Okay, Bob, stay calm and use the outdoor skills Pop taught you." I stared up at the top of the forty-foot-high pile of sawdust and thought from up there, I would have a good view of the whole area. First, I decided to walk around and see what I could find on the ground. I surveyed the entire yard, step by step, stopping to listen to the noises from the surrounding tree line. My heart skipped a beat when a woodrat dashed out from under a downed tree limb as I passed.

I made a complete circle around the huge sawdust pile and returned to my fire, where I warmed my hands and gulped another swallow of coffee to fortify myself. Like a magnet, the sawdust pile pulled at me, and I decided to climb to the top and look around. Luckily, the sawdust was packed down, and it was like climbing a sand dune, which I had plenty of experience doing over the years. I made it to the top, where it formed a broad mesa about thirty feet across. I inspected the area and found multiple tracks about the size of my hand that looked like a large cat's paw print. I could also see a smooth spot where the animal must have hunkered down. That's when a horrifying thought occurred to me—the beast might have been watching me throughout the night.

I knew big cats like bobcats and panthers were predators and often climbed to the highest position available to spot their prey. That spooked me, and I felt uneasy imagining what might have happened if it had considered me his prey. Pop and Uncle Charlie had told me stories about big cats that screamed like a woman. They said, "If you ever heard one, it would really unnerve you."

They were right about that. My mind returned to when I first saw the animal in my headlights and later heard that scream. A shiver ran through me as I imagined the big cat looking down on me from atop that sawdust pile. I couldn't wait to tell Pop and Grandma about my latest adventure.

Back at my campsite, I added more sticks to the fire and poured myself more coffee. I'd packed a peanut butter and jelly sandwich before I left, ate it, and sipped more coffee. There were squirrels here for the killing, but I had lost that hunting feeling and packed up my skeeter.

The thought of my close call with the panther lingered all the way home, teaching me a lesson about venturing into the woods alone.

EIGHT
Championship Basketball
"You can't do that"

There are only fifteen seconds left in the game. The Fletcher High Senators are leading, and our center, Claude Midgett, is inbounding the ball from the sideline. Coach Jarrett called the play during the timeout. Claude slaps the ball. That's our signal to run in different directions knowing the other team will guard us closely. Except I don't rush away willy-nilly. I spin around and circle wide toward our basket. Claude throws a high lob that bounces near the foul line. Perfect timing. I grab it and make a lay-up for the final two points of the game.

The buzzer sounds, and we go crazy because we have just won the Florida State Championship. My time with the Fletcher High basketball team ended with that game, but what a game and what a season it had been. That last play came from Coach Don Jarrett, who had shaped and guided our team throughout the season. He was not only a fine basketball coach but a man who believed in us and made us believe in ourselves.

I grew up loving sports. The challenge and the competition brought me a tremendous amount of enjoyment. Playing sports taught me always to give my best effort, play to win, but win fairly. As a father, I taught my children these important values about sports and life.

Growing up in our neighborhood, we played sandlot softball, baseball, and football. We'd race each other down the dirt roads just for fun. We played

Hide-and-Go Seek in the palmettos and woods surrounding our house, and when the neighborhood girls joined in, it became even more fun. All the kids in my neighborhood were from families in the same financial condition as we were. They didn't have money to spend on expensive toys, so our fun came from playing all kinds of sports and games together.

I played all sports, but I loved basketball and football the most.

When I was around ten, Pop helped me build a backboard and basketball hoop. He used a wire ring off a nail keg for the hoop, and Grandma sewed a net on it. We didn't have a pole but put it up with two-by-fours. At the city park, we measured the height of the hoop and the distance from the net to the free throw line. We used those measurements on my dirt basketball court, and now I was ready to start practicing.

Getting the ball in the net was a struggle at first, but over the next couple of years, as I grew stronger and taller, my basketball skills improved, and that net didn't seem so high or far away when I stood at the foul line.

I was out there shooting hoops whenever I had the time. When my friends came over, we practiced our shots and played pick-up games or competed in games of Horse. That homemade hoop was the main reason I ended the 1954 Fletcher High championship season with an 86% completion rate at the foul line. Because of my success, Coach Jarrett made me shoot all the technicals. I remember in one game, I had eighteen points from foul shots alone. He constantly pushed me to drive up the middle for a lay-up so I'd draw fouls.

I made the junior high basketball team in the eighth grade, but hunting and fishing were a high priority, and I missed so many practices Coach Scotty Henderson cut me from the team. Getting home from practice was also a problem because I rode the bus to school, and it was too late to catch the bus after practice. Peddling on those dirt roads helped me develop the leg power for rapid movement, adjusting to the flow of the game, and getting after the ball. I wasn't that fast, but I had quick reactions.

As much as I loved basketball, I didn't have the time to play very much in high school. Even after I'd built my skeeter and drove to school, I had to work to pay for upkeep and gas. So, again, practice was a problem. In sports, they say the best ability is availability, and working every day and on weekends made me unavailable. But things changed one day when Coach Brant pulled up to one of the pumps at Weber's garage where I worked. I ran out to fill up his car, and Mr. Brant, who was a friendly guy, started talking to me about school. He said, "Solano, you know this is your senior year. It's the last chance you'll have to play any sports. Why don't you get out there and play? The basketball team could use you."

"I wish I could, Mr. Brant," I said, "but I work every afternoon and can't attend practice."

He turned to Mr. Weber, who had wandered out to speak to his good customer. "Lou," he said, "can you let Solano off for a couple hours if he promises to come straight here after practice?"

Mr. Weber supported Fletcher High School, and his son Louis played on the team. Louis was one of my closest friends and in my same year at school. He was the reason I got the job at his dad's gas station. They were good folks. And because Mr. Brant asked him, he let me off every day for practice during my senior year.

Mr. Hoyt was the baseball coach and the 12th grade English teacher at Fletcher, but he also helped Coach Jarrett with basketball practice during the first part of the 1954 basketball season. One day when the bell rang, marking the end of the English class, Coach Hoyt cornered me. He said, "Solano, can you stay for a few minutes? I want to talk to you." All the coaches and teachers called me Solano, and at first, I thought I was in trouble, but he said he just wanted to talk with me alone.

He said, "Solano you have a lot of ability, but you're not using it. You're holding back and you need to turn it loose."

That was a shock. I said, "Coach, I didn't realize I was holding back."

"Watching you in practice it appears to me that you are a little insecure about doing something wrong when you're in the game," Coach Hoyt said.

I thought I'd been playing hard and following Coach Jarrett's instructions. "I don't want to get Coach Jarrett mad at me for doing something I shouldn't."

He shook his head and said, "Solano, don't worry about Coach Jarrett. You go out there and turn your ability loose. I'll talk with Coach Jarrett to be sure you have every opportunity to play with the first-string team. Go for it, Solano."

"Yes Sir. I will. I'll start today at practice, so help me."

Thanks to Coach Hoyt, I've been going for it in every part of my life. I have carried that conversation with me and always try to "Go for it" in whatever I do. He caught me at the right time, and his motivational talk inspired me to go out and play my best basketball for our team. I got so motivated and aggressive the team voted me to be the team captain. I'm not saying that I was the reason our team started winning, but after the team voted me to become their captain, I believe we won every game. We went through the regional and district tournaments and made it to the State Basketball Tournament in Gainesville.

WINNING THE DISTRICT CHAMPIONSHIP TOURNAMENT AGAINST STARKE HIGH

During that winning streak, we had some exciting games, but our game against Starke for the District Title stands out in my memory. Starke had a good team, and they had beaten us badly earlier in the season, but they were unprepared for the team we had become.

Their center was a big guy, maybe 6'4", and looked like he could play tight end on a pro football team. We knew he was Starke's leader and top scorer, averaging over thirty points a game. His teammates constantly fed him the ball around the basket, and he had a great hook shot. We weren't small, but he was bigger than any of us, so we knew we had to stop him from getting the ball as much as possible.

At practice, Coach Jarrett told us to arrive early on game day. When we got to the gym, he and Coach Hoyt had the blackboard setup, and they reviewed the strategy we'd need to contain Starke's center.

"Solano, on defense, you take their big guy and stick close to him all the time. Do your best to keep him from getting the ball. Midgett (Claude Midgett, our center), you stay between him and the basket. I want you breathing down his neck and slap the ball away if you can."

Next, he turned to Duane Burgess, our left forward, and said, "Move in on the big guy when he gets the ball and help Solano and Midgett bottle him up. I want you guys to double team him whenever they have the ball. You guys pick off their passes and look for David. He's going to be fast breaking on every play."

David Gard was one of the guards, and yes, Gard was his name.

We put our hands together and shouted "TEAM." You could feel the energy and resolve flowing through the entire team as we exited the locker room. The coach's plan worked, and we held the big guy to about ten points. You could see he was livid because we did such a good job defending and stealing the ball from him by double-teaming him front and back. After we'd scored sixteen points by stealing the ball and feeding it to Dave, they finally caught on and put a man on him.

The two teams went back and forth throughout the game, and with less than a minute left, Starke had tied the game. I glanced at the scoreboard—52–52 with fifty seconds left on the clock. Coach Jarrett called timeout. In the huddle, he told Dave to try and set me up to drive for a layup, hoping I'd get fouled. Duane was to follow me in for the rebound in case my shot missed.

David was our best ball handler and quickly brought the ball across the half-court line. I'm racing ahead on the other side of the court, and David made a perfect bounce pass to me. He rushed over to screen the man guarding me. I saw a clear path up the middle lane toward the basket and did my best impression of the future Michael Jordan, leaping past the free throw line to the basket. BAM! the big guy appeared out of nowhere and blocked my shot. The ball caromed out of bounds.

Fletcher ball.

Now there are only thirty seconds left in the game. Here comes the most exciting finish to any game I have ever played. Inbounding the ball, I used a play the coach had drawn up, and we'd practiced, but I never had a chance to try during a game. Here's what happened: The referee gave me the ball and blew the whistle. The big guy from Starke was guarding me close, his arms waving wildly as though sending semaphore signals. But the referee made him move back because he was standing on the in-bounds line.

He stepped away and turned his back to me to guard our players breaking for the ball. I have the ball in my hand, and the big guy's broad back is in front of me. I remembered the play. It seemed the perfect time to try it.

I bounced the ball off his back, and, as they say, fortune favors the brave. The ball bounced right back to me as I stepped in bounds. I made a reverse layup for two quick points in one smooth motion.

Our fans are going wild because I'd just put us in the lead. But the big guy is screaming like someone had pulled down his shorts. "You can't do that," he yelled.

The referee stepped in and explained that the ball was in play as soon as it contacted any offensive or defensive player in bounds. Then the ref pointed to the scorekeepers, signaling them to add two points for number 13, which was my number, and the scoreboard changed to 52–54, in our favor.

Starke's center lost his cool at this point and shouted at the referee. The ref spun around and tagged him with a technical, which made the big man even more furious. In the stands, the Starke fans were yelling obscenities at the ref, and I'm afraid there will be a riot. Starke's coach called a timeout to calm his center and plan their strategy for the last twenty-five seconds of the game.

Coach Jarrett huddled us up. My heart was beating wildly, and I'm sure the adrenaline was pumping in the rest of our team. Coach gets our attention.

"Listen up, guys. Solano, you shoot the technical. Everyone but David should be on the line to grab the rebound if Solano misses. David, you stay at the top of our key. If we get the rebound, heave it to David, who will take a shot if he can.

"Everybody clear on what we have to do? Okay, let's get it done."

We slap hands, and everyone breaks to head out on the court, but Coach Jarrett puts his hand on my shoulder. He holds me back and whispers in my ear. "Solano, do you hear our fans yelling *Solano can do it*? I want you to know that the entire team, including me, all those fans and all the pretty cheerleaders would appreciate it very much if you would go out there and make that technical."

For some reason, that made me laugh, but I jogged over to the foul line and dropped in another point. Starke inbounds the ball, and with our guards pressing them, they bring the ball down. Their guard glances at the clock and sees there are only ten seconds left. He heaves a Hail Mary from half court, hoping their center can get the rebound and make the shot before time runs out.

I'm off to the side trying to judge where the ball might come off the backboard, and I can see it's falling short. The other players stare at the backboard, waiting for it to hit so they can leap for the rebound. As the ball comes down, I jump up and grab it, look down court and see David waving his arms. I fling the ball as hard as I can the entire length of the court.

Somehow, David manages to catch it. Turning, he flips the ball toward the basket just as the buzzer goes off. The ball goes in. Game over. We win a barnburner, 57-52.

The Starke fans scream and throw things on the court. Our fans are wild with excitement because we won. Their fans are angry because they believed we cheated with the inbounds pass I bounced off their center's back. Someone called the Jacksonville Beach police to cool things down and clear the gymnasium. However, the crowd wasn't in a hurry to leave, and they continued fussing at each other. Luckily, no fights broke out, although there were a few later at Bill's Drive-In.

But what a finish to that game. No other game that season was as tight and as exciting. That win propelled us into the championship rounds, where we stayed in the Winner's Bracket and won every game including the final Championship game. Fletcher High School was crowned the 1954 Florida Basketball Champion in the AA Division.

I should give credit to my teammates because they were all fine players. Corky Borders at guard was a good outside shooter. If you didn't guard him closely, he could hurt you. David Gard, the other guard, was an excellent ball handler, dribbling with either hand and good on fast breaks. We always looked for him down court when we picked off a defensive rebound or stole the ball. I was the point guard; we played three men out. Claude Midgett, our center, wasn't tall by today's standards, maybe 6' 2", but he could grab those rebounds and won his share of jump balls. Duane Burgess played forward. He was an aggressive presence for the Senators on both offense and defense.

We had some damn good backups that played their hearts out when they got on the court. And our coach, Mr. Don Jarrett, was a fine coach. He was hard on us, but he was a warm guy on the inside, and we all loved him.

Robert "Bobby" Solano appeared prominently in the 1954 Duncan Fletcher High School yearbook that highlighted the championship basketball team, its team captain, and Bobby as Best Dancer.

PART FOUR

Bobby Moves on in Life Facing More Challenges

Bobby's Rules to Live by:

9. No one is in charge of your happiness but you.

10. Burn the candles, use the nice sheets, wear the fancy lingerie. Don't save it for a special occasion.
Today is that special day.

ONE

Sav-A-Stop Paves the Way
"Bob, slide over here to the driver's seat"

The week after graduating high school, I considered returning to my summer job digging ditches for the Jacksonville Beach Sewer Department until something better came along. Before I could grab a shovel and start flinging dirt, my friend Jim Minton called me. Jim and I had partied together and graduated in the same Fletcher High class.

"Hey Bobby," Jim said when I answered his call. "If you're interested in a good job with a lot of future growth, I can get you on with Sav-A-Stop." He told me Sav-A-Stop was a new company that Ernest Griffin and a few of his friends started. "And I believe it's going to grow fast," he added.

Jim had just started with Sav-A-Stop and was helping them find new employees. He said he could get me a job in the warehouse filling orders. I wasn't exactly sure what that meant, but it sounded a lot better than digging ditches. I thanked him for the opportunity and told him I was interested. "By the way," I said, "what does the job pay?"

"It starts at a dollar an hour," he said. And when I agreed, he told me to be there at seven in the morning.

I met Mr. Griffin the following day. He gave me a quick interview and hired me on the spot. He put me to work in the warehouse, and I learned about filling orders for the delivery trucks. But that didn't last long because Mr. Griffin called me to his office two days later. Griffin was a good old boy originally from Live Oak, Florida, who served in the navy during the war and in 1952 founded Sav-A-Stop, Inc. with J. V. Freeman and A. H. Edwards. Sav-A-Stop, as I quickly learned, specialized in selling and merchandising non-food products in health and beauty aids.

In his office, Mr. Griffin came right to the point. "We have an opening on our west route to Tallahassee and the guys recommended you to be a route salesman trainee. I want to take you out of the warehouse, and you can start route training."

I said that sounded great, and he said to be at the warehouse Saturday morning to help load the trainer's truck. "His name is Morris, and he runs the Charleston, South Carolina route."

That's how I met Morris Lupton, who became my lifelong friend until the day he died in 2019. That Saturday morning after we had loaded the truck, Morris said to be ready to go at 4:00 a.m. Monday morning. "We'll be gone until Friday night, so go see Mr. Griffin and get your expense advance. We get six dollars a day to eat and sleep on."

As I found out, a route salesman's job was to drive a big box truck loaded with health and beauty aids to deliver to grocery stores, mainly to A&P supermarkets at the time. A&P, Sav-A-Stop's first major customer, was located in almost every good-size Southeastern city. Morris's route took him north through Georgia with stops in Brunswick, Savannah, Augusta, and Macon. In South Carolina, we delivered products to Beaufort and Charleston A&Ps, turned around, and made stops at Cordele and Valdosta before returning to Jacksonville.

Morris was a hard-working son of a gun, and by the end of the first week, he had taught me the entire product line and the prices. He had developed a great relationship with our customers, and at almost every store, the clerks would help us put up our deliveries after checking us in.

I had only been riding with Morris a few days when we stopped at a red light on Victory Drive in Savannah. A nice-looking lady pulled up next to us on the driver's side and called to Morris. He must have known the lady because he said, "Bob, slide over here to the driver's seat and take the truck up to the A&P. It's just a couple of blocks on the right. When you get there, pull around to the delivery door in the back and I'll meet you there."

I had never driven that truck before and started to protest, but Morris opened his door and was gone. I'm thinking, you horny old rascal leaving me alone while you chase after that woman, but I had driven trucks with gears on the floor and slid over to the driver's seat. The A&P was right where Morris said it was, and soon I had backed the big truck up to the loading dock. Sure enough, Morris was there with the lady, who turned out to be the assistant manager.

She checked us in, helped us put the merchandise up, and we were out of there in an hour. Usually, that order would have taken us two to three hours to put up. As we pulled away to drive to our next stop, I said, "Morris, I think it's great that you have such good customer relations with these managers, but I got a bone to pick with you. Why the hell did you jump out of the truck and leave me when I had never driven the truck before? I don't think that's right."

Morris said, "Solano look, did they not tell you I was to train you on this route, including driving the truck?"

I said they did, and he said, "Okay, that was your first lesson on driving the truck." And he broke out in a laughing fit. That's the way things went between us after that.

Two weeks later, I was training with Hal Haliburton. The company promoted Hal to route supervisor and gave me his West Florida route. My advancement through the company moved just as swiftly as those first few weeks. I became a supervisor overseeing eight routes in Tallahassee. Then I was promoted to regional manager, district manager, and merchandising manager. My final title was Key Account Manager. I called on all the major chain headquarters for public relations and sales in this position.

I left the company eleven years later with an unbelievable education. I gained important experience by training people to take over positions when I moved on. These workplace experiences proved invaluable in my future enterprises. I'll never forget Mr. Griffin, who had faith in me and gave me the chance of a lifetime.

In my last few years with Sav-A-Stop, I opened several health and beauty aid outlets named Thrifty Discount Stores in Valdosta and Moultrie, Georgia. I worked on weekends to keep them running, taking my three oldest boys—Bucky, Danny, and Britt—with me. They were only six, seven, and eight years old and helped me put up stock and clean the stores.

With Jerry Rose, a close friend working at Sav-A-Stop, we opened two more stores in Leesburg and Lakeland, Florida. We had Sav-A-Stop's blessing because we bought all our merchandise from them, and they delivered it right to our stores. Leaving Sav-A-Stop was one of the most difficult decisions I'd ever made. I'd made great friends at Sav-A-Stop and had to consider my wife and five children who needed my support. My youngest son Brian was less than a year old at the time, but for some reason, I felt the need to keep moving forward and growing my own business. And as you'll see, I had a good reason to move on.

1962 photograph of the Sav-A-Stop Tallahassee division. Bobby Solano is seated on the left.

TWO
Supporting the Family
"Promise Me You'll be Somebody"

After I graduated high school and went to work at Sav-A-Stop, I was out of town five or six days a week but still living with Grandma and Pop. A few months after getting that job, I bought a Chevrolet two-door hard-top with the new V-8 engine, stick shift, and overdrive. My payments were $169 per month, exactly seventy-five percent of my monthly salary. But I wanted it, which was a good enough reason to buy it. That Chevy was the first new car in our family, and I was proud of it.

My mother and grandmother enjoyed nothing better than a Sunday drive in my new car, listening to the radio and drinking a few beers. I can still picture Grandma riding in the backseat with a beer in her hand, wearing my Fletcher High letterman's sweater with *State Champions* embroidered on it and a star with *Captain* below that. I realize now that what I had achieved up to that point—and I was just getting started—were important highlights in Grandma's and my mother's lives.

As I earned more money, I put a new roof on my mother's house. It had been leaking for several years, and the wood was rotten, so I had to replace the whole roof. I also paid off the loans Grandma had taken out to pay for lights and water during those times when Pop was out of work.

Grandma was the motivator in our little family. She kept us moving forward with her positive encouragement even in the hardest times. Everything she had gone through in her younger days had made her even stronger. Grandma would drink a few beers to get happy and say, this is like heaven compared to the Great Depression days and then have to keep everything together by herself after her husband, Pete (Pop to me), was away for four years in the Army Air Corps during World War II. She said, "I ate shit with the chickens sometimes in those days. But not anymore. My grandson has come to save the day."

She never asked me for money, though. She was very proud and believed in self-reliance. She never complained or shared their need for extra cash, and I had to pull it out of her. When I helped, she would get tears in her eyes and hug me hard and long.

I remember as a young boy, we would go to the store on Fridays to buy groceries and beer. Pop got paid on Fridays, and Grandma sometimes had to put a few items aside at the checkout counter because she didn't have enough money. But she always saved a dollar to play the lottery. She'd laugh and tell me how things would be different when she won the lottery. I can still see her laughing and drinking a beer, talking about all the things she wanted to do and things she would buy with that lottery money. One day after carrying on about winning the lottery, I noticed her eyes had teared up. As a nine-year-old boy, I thought she was happy thinking about all the good times to come when she won the lottery. I now understand she knew it was all a fantasy, a dream that would never come true.

I'm unsure why my family struggled so much. I guess they didn't know how to plan and save for the future. Whatever the reason, life was a tremendous struggle for my mother and grandmother.

I recall they set aside an entire day to do the wash. They would heat water over a wood fire in big black iron pots. After soaking the clothes, they used a scrub board to get the dirt out, then wrung them out by hand and hung them on a clothesline. It was like we lived in pioneer times because they both cooked on wood stoves. My job was to cut the wood and stack it in the wood pile for them. And they used metal flat irons heated on the stovetop to iron clothes.

On top of all her chores, Grandma always had a garden. If I close my eyes, I can still picture her working in the garden, wearing a big straw hat. I'd come home from school and find her turning up the soil with a shovel. Do you believe that?

We always ate well because of her hard work in the garden. She grew collards, cabbage, carrots, peas, tomatoes, and even potatoes. She would can the extra vegetables in mason jars for the winter and sometimes salt down the fish we caught in salt barrels. But none of us liked fish that way, so she didn't do that very often. She made homemade wine from her grape vines. She always told me to shoot the birds off her grapes with the BB gun. "And shoot any crows that are in the garden too," she'd yell after me.

Where was the money going to come from in those days? My mother cleaned a few houses in the neighborhood and washed clothes for neighbors to earn a few dollars. It didn't add up to much because all our neighbors were as broke as we were. I remember my grandmother telling me, "Son, I want you to promise me that when you grow up, you'll be somebody, so you don't have live like us. Get a good job, save some of your money every week, even if it is only one dollar. You need to save! Please, promise me you will be somebody. Promise me right now," she insisted.

I said, "Yes, Grandma. I promise."

She hugged me real tight, and her eyes glistened with tears.

After I grew up, I realized how momma and Grandma must have felt with all the pressure and the hurt they had endured. There must be a special place in heaven for them. But I was intent on keeping my promise, and ICEE paved the way.

THREE

The First Challenge Comes My way —
ICEE, The Frozen Drink You Eat
"You need to see for yourself"

During my Key Account job with Sav-A-Stop, I had the opportunity to meet the owners of many convenience store chains, including these Florida entrepreneurs: Mr. Robert Jaeb, Shop & Go stores in Tampa, Lewis Huntley, Jiffy Food stores in Orange Park, George Miller, Handy Food Stores in Crescent City, W.C. Jones, in Crestview, and many more.

I saw an unusual sight on one trip to call on the district manager at Pac-A-Sak in Pensacola. Driving up to their office, next door to one of their stores, I noticed two lines of people lined up at the store's front doors. In all my visits to convenience stores, I had never seen people lining up to get inside. Seeing lines of people was so strange I had to find out what was happening. Inside the store, I observed both clerks dispensing drinks from two identical machines behind the check-out counter. I could see it was a drink that appeared more solid than liquid, almost like ice cream.

The two clerks were filling up the cups and serving customers so fast the dispensers couldn't keep up. The sign on the machines indicated that one machine was for cherry flavor and the other for cola. That was my introduction to ICEE, the "frozen carbonated beverage."

The story of the ICEE product is a fascinating one that I'll share since it became a big part of my success. In 1958, Omar Knedlik, the owner of a Dairy

Queen franchise in Coffeyville, Kansas, was forced to store his soda bottles in the freezer after his cooler broke down. The freezer created a slush-like concoction, thanks to the drinks' high sugar content, and the soda would instantly turn to slush when customers opened the bottles. His customers lapped them up like crazy. Knedlik decided to try to make his own soda freezing machine to chill and dispense the drinks by jury-rigging a contraption from an automobile air conditioning unit. He had first called his new beverage Scoldasice (Get it? "Cold as ice"), but Knedlik's friend Ruth E. Taylor, a local artist, came up with the new name and the company logo. Knedlik partnered with the John E. Mitchell Company in Dallas to develop the machine, and a national phenomenon was born.

Knedlik introduced the machines to selected convenience stores in the early 1960s, when I saw my first ICEE machine in Pensacola. I had become friendly with W.C. Jones, who owned the Junior Food Stores in Crestview, Florida. We had talked about working together and possibly opening convenience stores in South Georgia. No one had opened a chain of convenience stores in the Valdosta, Georgia area where I had my Thrifty Discount Stores, and it seemed like a good market.

After seeing how popular the ICEE machine was, I went straight to the phone and called him. "W.C.," I said. "There's something you need to see right away. I'm in Pensacola at the Pac-A-Sak store next to their office. Do you know where that is?"

He said he did. "I'll be there as fast as I can if you think it's that important, but what is it?"

"It's hard to explain. You need to see for yourself."

Crestview was about an hour away from Pensacola, and I watched dozens more people buying ICEEs as I waited for him to arrive. When W.C. saw the ICEE machines in action, he became as excited as I was, saying, "Wow, I need them in my stores, Bob."

We copied the company's phone number off the machines and called them from the store. We made an appointment to meet with Fred Montalvo of Southern ICEE headquarters in Baton Rouge, Louisiana, to see how we could get machines for W.C.'s stores and a possible franchise if one were available.

Life was about to make some dramatic turns on my path to success.

FOUR

Life-Changing Decision Comes in a Frozen Cup
"Will you put that in writing for Bob?"

We arrived in Baton Rouge the next morning to meet with Fred Montalvo, President of the Southern ICEE Beverage Corporation. His secretary had told us he was the man to talk to about ICEE franchises in Florida and Georgia.

Montalvo was not in office when W.C. and I entered the office, but his secretary said he shouldn't be long. An hour later, we were still waiting when Tom Devine, President of National ICEE, approached us and apologized for making us wait so long. He said he knew where Fred was and left to find him. They returned together thirty minutes later.

Montalvo was aware of our interest in obtaining a franchise for the ICEE machines. Still, he seemed indifferent as he told us Florida was out of the question because he had already signed a contract with the 7-Eleven stores and committed his allotment of machines. At the time, 7-Eleven had over 300 stores in Florida and was opening one or two a week. He did offer to sell us a franchise for Georgia but stated it would be over a year or even two before we could get any machines.

This was not what we were hoping to hear. Montalvo went on to explain that his allotment of machines was only twenty per month, but the manufacturer, the John E. Mitchell Company in Dallas, was working hard to expand production. That was a bit of good news. But not much. He told W.C. that since we had come all that way and 7-Eleven had no stores in the West Florida area, he would get him at least one ICEE dispenser every two weeks until the company manufactured more machines. But he said it might take a year or two before he'd have enough for all his stores.

We learned that Devine and Montalvo had obtained what the Mitchell Company called a Developer franchise for the ICEE machines, which allowed them to sell and lease machines to Sub-Developers. Devine's and Montalvo's Southern ICEE Beverage Corp. had first been granted franchise rights only in Louisiana, Mississippi, Alabama, and parts of Florida. Several months later, they acquired the rights to southeastern Texas, all of South Carolina, and the remainder of Florida.

By October 1965, the partners received the rights to ICEE equipment for most of the remaining geographical United States, and the original contract was terminated. The two executives had problems working together and decided to split their territories equally. The new franchise agreement gave Montalvo all the states east of the Mississippi, and Devine had all the states west of the Mississippi. They also split their allotment of machines 50/50, giving them each twenty machines per month.

Tom Devine had sat silently throughout our meeting with his former part-ner, and when the meeting was over, Devine said he wanted to talk with us in his office. Montalvo said his goodbyes and departed, and we moved to Devine's office.

Devine opened up to us and said the ICEE Company had not committed all his machines yet, and he was busy laying out his overall operation plan. "I want to open up markets in Fort Worth, Texas, Las Vegas, Los Angeles, and Salt Lake City," he told us. "And I need an operations manager to help me plan everything and head up the daily operations."

He had already signed contracts with 7-Eleven to install ICEE machines in all their stores in the major cities he'd named and the surrounding communities.

I could see the size of the job he faced weighed on him, and he had some-thing in mind, so I encouraged him to keep talking.

"I'm just getting started," he said. "Now, we need to hire a lot of people, rent offices and warehouses, and get everything moving. All of that needs to be done before we start installing the machines in all those 7-Eleven stores."

No doubt it was a big job, but he had already hired a service manager for the Fort Worth region and signed a lease on a warehouse with a small of-fice. The service manager he hired was coming to Baton Rouge for training the following week. We found this all interesting, and I hoped it was leading up to the offer of a franchise. He dropped a surprise on us with his next statement.

"Bob, W.C., you both impressed me, and I think we can help each other and make some money together. I'll sell you a Sub-Developer franchise if we can make a deal."

Naturally, we were interested, and I asked him what kind of deal he had in mind.

"You can buy a franchise in any of the cities in my area, but I want you, Bob, to come and work for me as my operations manager for one year."

The franchise would cost us $5,000 for each machine we bought, up to 35. After that, Devine would lower the price to $2,500 per machine. He said he was selling all his franchises based on fifty machines at $5,000 each, but he would give us a break if I accepted his job offer. Devine said he'd pay me $250 a week and all my expenses to move my family from Florida to Baton Rouge.

I was currently making $200 a week with Sav-A- Stop, and I probably wouldn't consider switching jobs for the extra fifty dollars, but the franchise deal made it almost irresistible.

W.C. said, "Will you put that in writing for Bob?"

"Of course, I will," Devine replied.

"Tom, that sounds like a fair offer," I said, "but I'll need to discuss it with W.C. on our way back to Crestview. And, of course, with my family. How about I give you an answer in one week?"

He agreed and said to let him know as soon as I decided. "You can see from what I've shared with you that time is of essence for our company. We must begin setting up the machines and start shipping them to these areas. There's a lot of work to do."

I told him I understood and would get back to him within the week. We shook hands, and W.C. and I began our nine-hour drive back to Crestview. We immediately started reviewing the pros and cons of Devine's offer. W.C. began by saying, "Bobby, I know this is a big move for you to make. I don't know how good it will be for you and your family and for us in the franchise. But whatever you decide, I will back you up. If things blow up, me and Miss Earline have enough room in our house for you and the family, till we find you a job."

We laughed, and he added, "But all kidding aside, I'll bet you a gold dollar that Sav-A-Stop will take you back in a New York minute."

He was right about Sav-A-Stop. When I told Mr. Griffin about my offer, he said, "Bob, the door is always open for you. I wish all the best of luck to you and the family."

FIVE
Moving to Baton Rouge with National ICEE Corporation
"Things were coming together quickly"

At home, my wife Diane didn't have much to say except she wanted to visit her family in Phoenix. Our kids were all under ten years old and didn't understand the move. Quite frankly, I don't believe they cared where we lived as long as there were nearby ball fields and basketball courts.

I called Tom Devine and told him I was coming and would be there the following Sunday. He was more than delighted to know I'd accepted his offer. On Monday morning, I met with Tom and his secretary, and we began what turned into an intensive three-day seminar on the workings of the ICEE National Beverage Company.

I'd contacted a Baton Rouge realtor, and after leaving the ICEE office each day, we spent hours looking at houses. I'd told him about our large family, and he called me the second day and said, "Bob, I found just what you are looking for. We can see it tonight."

It turned out to be just what I wanted—a three bedroom, two bath house and of all places, it was located next to a city park. I knew my guys would go crazy playing out there every day and with me on weekends. I bought it on the spot.

The next day I flew into Dallas Love Field, and Arthur, the Fort Worth Service Manager, picked me up. Arthur was a big guy with a good attitude and seemed willing to work. He took me to the 7-Eleven stores, and I saw they were already preparing the counters for the ICEE machines, installing water lines and electricity hook-ups. Anticipating the arrival of the first twenty machines, Arthur had ordered the ICEE supplies of cups, straws, and syrups.

The ICEE is a carbonated beverage made of flavored syrup (with lots of sugar), water, and carbon dioxide. The machine is where the magic happens, and each one requires a canister of CO_2 for the carbonization process. Arthur told me we'd meet with the CO_2 man the next morning at our office.

The service manager had made good progress. The Baton Rouge home office had already provided him with a pickup truck with a liftgate to carry the machines to the stores. Arthur said he had three or four people coming in for interviews the next day, adding, "But I need to know who to contact in the home office for supplies and parts for machines. Do you have names and phone numbers for me?"

I told him I had everything he needed and would go over evverything with him and leave him copies of everything. He was most appreciative and said he'd been a bit lost all by himself. The next day I hired a secretary and a route trainee, and while Arthur was organizing the tools on his truck, the shipment of cups and straws arrived.

Things were coming together quickly. We worked out the schedule for the CO_2 man to drop tanks at the first twenty stores that morning. Before I arrived, I had asked Arthur to pick up a large map of the Fort Worth metropolitan area and a box of thumb tacks. I was happy to see he already had the map mounted on a wall with all the store locations pinned on the map. We picked the first twenty stores closest to our office and made a route schedule for our delivery days.

We worked over the weekend organizing our desks and reviewed the billing invoice books and route sheets for everyone. I gave them a list of people to call in the main office for questions on billing, machine parts, and ordering supplies.

Monday morning, we met with 7-Eleven's local district manager, showed him the locations we'd selected for his first machines, and reviewed the operating procedures with him. We took the route trainee with us for the exposure and discussed our operations with him while we drove to the meeting. The first fifteen machines came in late Monday evening, and the next morning we loaded the machines and supplies and delivered them to the first stores.

At the stores, we showed the clerks how to operate and serve the ICEE drinks. After placing ICEE signs with the distinctive logo in the store windows, spent the rest of the afternoon working with the clerks to serve ICEEs to customers. We used this same procedure in every store throughout Fort Worth and all the other cities we added to the franchise line.

The following day, I bought a copier and other supplies for the office. Arthur took me to the airport at about 2:00 p.m., and I caught a plane to Vegas, where I started putting together our Las Vegas franchise.

My first meeting in Vegas was with the 7-Eleven district manager. He took me to one of the stores that were already wired and plumbed for the ICEE machine. He told me his employees were busy working on the rest of the stores. I told him he was doing a great job. He also took me to a strip shopping center with several vacant spaces for rent. The location and the office space checked all the boxes, and I called the rental agent. But that wasn't the end of the district manager's helpfulness. He told me about his brother-in-law, Mike, a young man working for a large electric company looking for another job with a better future. He strongly recommended his brother-in-law but told me he wouldn't get mad if I didn't hire him.

That sounded too good to be true, so I called Mike, and we arranged to meet for breakfast. I gave Mike the application papers to fill out and asked him to drop them off at my motel since we didn't have a working office yet. I told him I'd review his work history and run a credit report before getting back to him. He understood it would be two weeks before we would need him to start, which was fine with him since he wanted to give the electric company his notice.

In short order, I leased one of the vacant store locations, and after reviewing Mike's application and meeting with him once more, I hired him to be the Las Vegas ICEE Service Manager. I couldn't believe the way everything had fallen into place so quickly.

The next day I met Mike at the building we had leased and discussed possible layouts for storing the supplies. I informed him that the first machines would arrive in about two weeks, but whether they were here or not, he would go on salary in two weeks. I gave him a list of our personnel at the home offices with phone numbers and how to reach me.

We had made a lot of progress, and I left on Friday and flew back to Fort Worth to see how things were going. On Saturday, Arthur and I visited all the stores with the new ICEE machines to be sure everything was working correctly and answer any questions the salesclerks might have. I was happy to see they were pumping out ICEEs at a brisk rate. I worked with our people Monday, Tuesday, and Wednesday before catching a flight back to New Orleans and on to the Baton Rouge home office, where I reported to Tom on our progress.

I was pleased with how everything had come together but surprised that Tom seemed to be a little annoyed and reminded me to be sure everyone was following his instructions and not mine. He ended the meeting rather abruptly, and I left, not thinking too much about it.

Later I checked with Arthur in Fort Worth and then called Mike, my new Las Vegas Service Manager, filling them in on what I'd learned at Monday's operations meeting. Mike was excited about the new job and thanked me for hiring him. I also called the Salt Lake City 7-Eleven district manager to let him know I'd be there in two weeks, informing him when the machines would arrive, and we could begin installations. He told me they would have over half of his stores ready with electricity and water. He had thirty-seven stores in Salt Lake City and six more in Provo.

After telling him how pleased I was with the progress he'd made and that

I was looking forward to meeting him, I hung up and moved on to the next piece of important business—closing on our new house in Baton Rouge. Our furniture would be picked up Wednesday, and I'd drive the family to Baton Rouge the next day. Hopefully, we'd be there when our belongings arrived.

On top of all this, I was still running my Thrifty Discount Stores in Georgia, or I should say my employees were running them for me. I spoke with the store managers almost daily and mailed their paychecks each week from wherever I was at the time. I discovered that the managers placed bets on what postmark would be on the envelopes each week. None of this would have worked if I didn't have honest and reliable managers. I even trusted them to make the daily cash deposits. I carried the Thrifty Discount Stores' checkbook everywhere I went so I could write their paychecks and pay bills from wherever my ICEE job took me. It was an interesting time, to say the least.

Back in Jacksonville, I embraced my family again. I had been so busy that I didn't realize how much I had missed them and cried myself to sleep with happiness. At breakfast, it felt almost like I'd never left. My boys were thrilled that their dad was back, and I told them, "You guys are going to love our new home in Baton Rouge. Our backyard is right next to the city park with sports fields and playground equipment. All the neighborhood kids come there to play after school and on the weekends."

I wanted Diane to know I had found a special place for her and the kids. I looked forward to having four days together before we left for Louisiana.

We arrived in Baton Rouge on Friday morning, and the moving van was waiting for us at our new house. After the movers unloaded the furniture, my boys wanted to see the park. I told them to go ahead since it was basically across the street. They played there until dark, and I had to go get them for dinner.

I was home the entire weekend and showed Diane the boy's school, which was only two blocks away. I believed I had found the perfect neighborhood for us with the park, the school, and a shopping center only a mile away.

***

Tom Devine met with all his employees every Monday, whether I was in town or not. This Monday, Tom let us know that we would receive extra machines over the next couple of months in addition to our usual allotment of twenty machines. He explained it was because the Mitchell Company had already shipped a hundred machines to Florida when he and Fred Montalvo split. So, Tom's National ICEE Company was getting additional machines to match the number Fred already had in his Southern ICEE company. That meant Fort Worth would receive thirty machines, and another twenty were on the way to Vegas.

I phoned our people in Fort Worth and Las Vegas to share the good news about the extra machines and that I'd be back in Fort Worth for a couple of days this week. From there, I flew to Vegas and helped Mike install the first machines. He'd received all the ICEE supplies, and I worked with him for a few days.

In Vegas, Mike and I took our time organizing the office and the small warehouse. Then we loaded up the truck to begin installations first thing in the morning. We hit three or four 7-Elevens in a row, and the installations went smoothly. Mike and I spent a lot of time training the clerks over the next two days. Mike was a great worker, and as an electrician, he was knowledgeable about the electrical connections and tools needed for the job. He also worked well with the 7-Eleven people.

I was amazed at how quickly he had picked up the entire installation procedure, and at one point, he said, "Boss, I got this. Why don't you help some of the others who need more help?"

That was a relief knowing I had someone I could rely on, and on Saturday, I caught a plane to Salt Lake City. The 7-Eleven district managers were friendly and cooperative in every one of our franchise cities. They were excited to get the ICEE machines after hearing so much about them from their home office. I found the district manager in Salt Lake City to be no exception. He was a great guy and took me on a tour of his stores, showing me the installation work they had done. He also shared some interesting information.

"Bob, look at our candy department," he said. "Compared to other district stores our candy sales are the highest in the entire 7-Eleven chain of stores. We have more space devoted to candy as you can see. And look at our cooler displays. We devote a lot of space to flavored soft drinks and juices, but not so much to colas and caffeine drinks as in 7-Eleven's other districts."

"Why is that?" I asked.

"It's because we're in a predominantly Mormon and Catholic area. Neither church believes in birth control for one thing. I think the average family size is about six point two with children. In addition, most Mormons stay away from caffeinated beverages, and they teach their children not to use them. But they do drink a lot of the flavored sodas."

That was news to me, but I could see the district manager had done his homework.

"What I'm trying to say is I think we're going to need two machines in a few of the stores to keep up. I believe we're going to blow the roof off ICEE sales per store." He broke into a smile and added, "We'll give the other districts something to talk about."

He said he was tired of hearing stories of how the ICEE machines were pumping up profits in other districts. "We may all work for the same company, but there's always a friendly competition going on. It keeps us on our toes."

WE FIND OUR ICEE FRANCHISE

After this conversation, I couldn't wait to get on the phone with my partner. "W.C., I found the franchise we want. It's Salt Lake City, Utah." I could barely contain my excitement, but W.C. wasn't convinced.

He laughed at my suggestion and said, "Bob, that's on the other side of the world. Why would we want to go way out there?"

I explained to him what the Salt Lake City district manager had told me, and he became just as excited as I was. "Let's do it," he said. "I believe in you,

Chief." That was his nickname for me.

Back at the home office, Tom Devine was getting deeper in debt, borrowing money for his business operations and expanding into the Fort Worth and Las Vegas markets. W.C. and I told him we were interested in Salt Lake City for our franchise, explaining that it had just the number of stores we thought we could adequately support with two people and a part-time person in the office to do all our paperwork. We let him know we were anxious to start our operation but didn't share any information I'd learned from the district manager.

Tom had no problem assigning us the Salt Lake City franchise since this was part of the agreement when he hired me. He was probably relieved because it saved him from all the expenses needed to open another market. He'd be fulfilling his contract with 7-Eleven while collecting his share of machine and supply fees without doing all the work since W.C. and I would be putting out the cash investment for the whole Salt Lake City franchise.

I considered it to be a win-win deal all the way around. Our good fortune continued when Devine told me of a young man named Danny working in the John E. Mitchell Company in Dallas who wanted to go outside as a service manager for one of the ICEE franchises. He came highly recommended and already had a clean background check. After another conversation with his current employer, I called Danny and hired him over the phone. We wouldn't need to train him in the operation of the machine since he knew the ICEE machine inside and out.

Danny said he was single and could be in Salt Lake City a couple of weeks after giving his notice at the plant the next day. Now we were in business. I found a warehouse and office in Salt Lake City about three blocks from the 7-Eleven district office and leased it. I gave Danny the address and told him he could bunk in the warehouse for a few days until he found an apartment. I advised him to borrow one of his mother's mattresses and bring some blankets, as it was cool there. That made his day. He said he was excited and ready to go.

I ordered supplies for the Salt Lake City franchise, contacted the local CO_2

retailer, and put a sign in our office window advertising for a route driver, adding the Baton Rouge office number. We received two calls before I returned to the home office.

I couldn't believe we had been lucky enough to land a franchise for what could be one of the hottest sales markets in the country. W.C. called and said he had reviewed the franchise agreement with Tom Devine, and it should be ready for us to sign this Monday morning at Tom's office. I caught a plane back to New Orleans the next day. It was Thursday, and I was glad to be with my family again. Diane told me she had made most of the arrangements for the boy's school registrations, and I enjoyed a long weekend playing with the boys and eating home-cooked meals.

At our Monday department meeting, I brought everyone up to date on operations at the three franchise locations. After the meeting, I met with each department head to follow up on orders of supplies for all three of our ICEE operations.

Arthur was making significant progress in Fort Worth. He'd received the second order of machines and was halfway through the installation process with no problems. Since Arthur and his people were moving right along, I decided to head back to Vegas to give Mike a hand. He was still a one-man operation, although Tom had given me permission to hire another person. I intended to do that while I was there. Mike already had someone in mind, and we hired him. Over the last two weeks, Mike and I installed all fifteen machines and were waiting for more.

I took the time to check in with the Las Vegas 7-Eleven district manager, who reported all the machines were working well. He said Mike had kept him informed on everything, and all they needed now was more machines installed. "So, get off the phone, Bob, and help Mike install more machines."

We both got a laugh out of that.

I spent the rest of the week working with Mike and Joe, the new man, to install the last couple of machines. We also visited every store to check their supplies and build our relationships with the store clerks. The rest of the time, I worked with Joe and Mike to be sure they understood each store's service procedures. I showed them how to report weekly service routes and installations in their procedure book and instructed them to always speak to the manager or the clerks when they arrived and let them know they were there to check the ICEE supplies in the back room.

Here's how the service procedures were detailed in the ICEE Company rule book.

- Write up the order and get the supplies from the truck.
- Have the clerk check supplies and sign the invoice.
- Put up supplies and straighten up all the cups and syrup in the back room.
- Fill up the two syrup containers in the machine for clerks and wipe down the machine.
- Defrost the machine to stop any ice build-up in the machine and make sure both sides are working before you leave.

I left on Friday morning for New Orleans and home.

Monday morning's meeting went well, though Tom was a little upset because I had returned so soon. "It's too expensive to fly in and out each week," he complained.

"Yes sir, it is expensive," I agreed, "but with all due respect, it may be more cost-effective when you consider staying over the weekend and the cost of meals and motel rooms."

Tom didn't appreciate my reasoning and said, "There you go again, not wanting to follow my orders."

I started to reply, but he cut me off. "Never mind, just do as I say. Now let's finish this Salt Lake City franchise agreement for you and W.C." He asked his secretary to stay in the office, and we called W.C. and discussed it briefly. There were no problems with the contract, and Tom and I signed it. The secretary put it in the mail overnight to W.C.

I left the office early for home and flew to Vegas the following day to check things out with Mike and Joe. Mike was pleased with his route man and said it appeared that 7-Eleven's operations and sales were excellent. Overall, the operations in both cities were doing quite well, especially after we added the new men. But I was not happy being away from my family so much. I hoped I could do something to eliminate the amount of traveling, although I knew Tom would have a problem with that. I did get a lucky break when Devine sold the Los Angeles franchise the same week I arrived for work. Otherwise, my travel schedule would have been even crazier.

Back in Salt Lake City for two weeks, I helped Danny set up the office and organize the operations. I'd hired another man to help him with the installations, and they were making good progress. The new man was also trained as a route driver and would service the 7-Eleven stores with weekly supplies.

We received another twenty machines, as Tom had promised, and Danny began installing those machines. I think he was probably the best all-around service manager I had hired, and glad he was working for our franchise. Danny had twelve or thirteen machines already installed when the second shipment arrived. He'd been working nonstop, including weekends. I told him, "Danny, you don't have to work the full weekend. At least take Sunday off."

He smiled and shook his head, saying, "Boss, I would rather be working than sitting around doing nothing. Our new man likes making the overtime too."

I flew home Friday morning.

Monday after Tom's meeting, I received a frantic call from Danny about badly needing syrup and cups. The volume of ICEE sales in each store was unbelievable, and the Salt Lake City stores were running out of supplies. I worked on updating our supply order and taking care of some other business the rest of the day and flew back to Salt Lake City the next day.

Danny was still bunking in the warehouse, but he had found a small apartment over a couple's garage. He told me it suited him well and wasn't very expensive. At work, he had completed installing machines in about thirty-eight stores and planned to finish the last of the Salt Lake stores that week and move on to the six in Provo.

Danny and I visited with the 7-Eleven district manager to be sure he was pleased with how everything was working. My years with Sav-A-Stop showed me the value of staying close to a store's management team and building strong relationships with them. The district manager told us what I wanted to hear, that everything was good. He said his people told him Danny was responding to their calls, and if his store managers were happy then he and his supervisors were happy.

But he had a suggestion. "You may want to increase the cases of syrup in some of the stores that are selling extremely well," he said. "Danny, I'm sure you know the ones I'm talking about."

Danny said, "Yes, sir," and named five stores near schools. The manager said, "There's such a demand for ICEEs in three or four of those stores that the store managers have to lock the doors after school and only let so many school children in at a time, because they can't watch them all. And the machine won't keep up with the demand either."

Danny suggested we could add another machine in one or two of the stores. The district manager agreed but said, "Let's give it another week or two and see how things go."

I spent the rest of my week riding with Danny and his route man, visiting stores, checking our supplies, and working with the 7-Eleven clerks to be sure they knew as much about the operation of the machines as we did.

I was working as hard as I ever had, but it had been smooth sailing so far. That was about to change.

SIX
Take the Faucets Off
"We have to teach them a lesson"

I called Arthur Thursday night while waiting for my connecting flight from Dallas to New Orleans to be sure everything was going smoothly in the Fort Worth market. Instead of the usual good news, Arthur reported a problem we hadn't anticipated. He said when his route man arrived at the first 7-Eleven store that morning, the manager accepted all the supplies except the syrup. The store manager told the route man that from now on, they would order their syrup from Velda, the dairy company owned by 7-Eleven.

Arthur said he tried to reach me that morning but couldn't and called Mr. Devine. He said, "Sorry about that, boss, I kinda wish I hadn't."

I could tell he felt terrible about it and assured him it wasn't a problem. "What did Tom say?" I asked.

"Mr. Devine said to have my man take both faucets off so they couldn't use the machines. I was shocked, and asked him if he meant to take the faucets off the machines in every store on the route? And he said 'Yes. Take them off now. We have to teach them a lesson.'"

Tom's orders had created a crisis, and I told Arthur I needed to stay and help with the problem. "Do you mind driving to the Dallas airport and picking me up?"

On the way to the Fort Worth motel where I usually stayed, Arthur provided me with more details about his conversation with Tom. Having been on the receiving end of Tom's autocratic directives, I understood why Arthur was so upset. I told him not to worry and to get some rest tonight. "But be sure to call your route man and tell him not to leave the warehouse tomorrow morning until we meet with him."

I called Tom first thing the next morning and advised him against taking such drastic action as removing the faucets from the machines. "We should first try to meet with their top management and try to negotiate this situation."

Tom was having none of it. "I gave an order, and I expect those faucets to be removed. Why are you even questioning this?"

"Tom, I'm afraid this could jeopardize the relationship with our only major customer."

He didn't look at it that way and thought playing hardball was the way to go. "Listen to me, Bob. They can't get ICEE machines from anywhere else so they will come around. Just do as I have instructed you!" And he hung up.

Within minutes the phone started ringing. My first thought—or hope—was that Tom had changed his mind. Instead, the call was from the local 7-Eleven district manager. He was very composed and asked me what was going on. After I explained the situation to him, he said, "Well, Bob, I got orders this morning from the home office, the top brass. They said if your people remove any more faucets from the machines, we are to disconnect the water and electricity, roll the ICEE machines outside, and leave them on the sidewalk. We are to refuse all deliveries from ICEE, and we want all those machines picked up and off our sidewalks within the next ten days."

I quickly tried to calm the situation. "There's no need for that," I said, "I'll make sure the faucets aren't removed. I may not be employed after that, but I'll take care of it."

He laughed at that, and I joined him, but I was deadly serious. My job security was on the line knowing how Tom hated for anyone to go against his orders. But that was what I was about to do.

My stomach churned as I placed a call to my boss. "Tom," I said, "We have a little more of a problem regarding removal of the faucets."

Once again, he cut me off. "I really don't want to discuss this issue any-more," he said.

But I persisted. "This is important, Tom. I've just spoken with the Fort Worth 7-Eleven district manager, and he told me that if we take any more faucets off their ICEE machines, they have orders to disconnect the lines and roll the machines out on the sidewalk and stop all deliveries to their stores. The district manager said he thought this had come from Mr. Jerry Thompson him-self." Thompson was the president and one of the majority owners at 7-Eleven.

Tom didn't respond to that, and I pushed on, "You may not like what I'm saying, but if you value our relationship with 7-Eleven, I'd suggest you call Mr. Thompson immediately. We have stopped removing the faucets and won't take any action until I hear back from you."

Tom must have realized the seriousness of the situation and said, "I'll call you back in the next hour."

I hung up the phone and turned to Arthur. "We bought us a little time," I said. "Everything's on hold for at least an hour."

Tom's office manager called within the hour and told us to replace the faucets and continue our services. When I asked to speak to Tom, the office manager said he'd left the building and would talk to me tomorrow.

I instructed Arthur and the route driver to put the faucets back on the machines. Arthur was relieved, but worried about how Tom would react to the situation. "I don't think Tom is pleased with us about how this all went down, Bob. I don't want to lose my job."

I told him not to worry because the responsibility was all mine. "As of now, I'm still the vice president of operations. I don't think Tom understood that we had no other choice but to try and repair the relationship with our only customer. They had us over a barrel, and I made the decision to stop removing the faucets. As soon as they're back on, I'll call the district manager and let him know we won't be removing any more. I'm sure he'll appreciate it and pass the news on to the rest of his people."

We took both trucks and began servicing the stores with supplies and mending fences. We continued replacing faucets and delivering supplies until late in the afternoon.

***

Arthur had mentioned something to me while driving between the stores that got my attention. He said the 7-Eleven stores in the Dallas district were testing a different machine than our ICEE machine. One of the 7-Eleven store supervisors had told him they couldn't get ICEE machines fast enough and wanted to try the new dispensers. They were promoting the new product as Slurpee. Art had seen the Slurpee machine in the store next to the 7-Eleven district office. The manager told him not to worry about it because the product was not as good as our ICEE product. Trouble alarms were ringing in my head, despite what the district manager had told Art, but I didn't let on. I said, "We need to see that machine and the product right now."

We pulled up to the store, and I asked Art if he had a sweater or jacket he could put on over his ICEE shirt. "I want us to look like a couple of customers fascinated by the machine and the Slurpee drink, so they won't be suspicious after we buy a couple of big ones and ask a few questions."

After he put on his jacket, we entered the store, and I took the first steps in another chapter of my life story.

THE SLURPEE MACHINE

They served the Slurpees behind the front counter from a dispenser with a trademark *Taylor Machine* emblem attached to the front. We both commented on the new product and bought a large cup each. After slurping a mouthful (and that's where 7-Eleven came up with the name—the sound of the "slurp" people made when drinking it), I said to the young clerk, "Mmm, this is good. How long have ya'all had this?"

She said about a month.

"What makes it stand up like ice cream in the cup? And it tastes great. Just like wild cherry."

She was eager to explain the process to us. "It's a special mixture of syrup and water, and the machine carbonates the drink, just like a Coke or Pepsi."

She spoke proudly, like a schoolgirl who had won a spelling bee. "If you are wondering how I know this," she said, "it's because the man that installed the machine trained me, and 7-Eleven is using our store to train all newly hired employees. So, I've repeated it about a thousand times to curious customers like you."

I thanked her for taking the time to explain it to us and asked if she knew how the syrup and water got to the machine.

"See those hollow, plastic lines going into the machine," she said, pointing to the lines. "The lines come from the back room where they are hooked up to five-gallon syrup cans that we keep full. The CO_2 pushes the syrup to the machine from those cans into what they call a carbonator in the bottom of the machine. The carbonator blends the mixture for the drink then sends it up to these hoppers." She opened a lid on the machine to show us the hopper. "This is where the mixed product is pre-cooled then it goes down into the freezing chambers and freezes the product as you dispense it out of the freezing chambers through one of these faucets."

"You really know your stuff, honey, and I can't thank you enough for explaining it so clearly. I can now say I know how a Slurpee is made. Who makes the machines, by-the-way? Is there a name plate on the back?"

She looked and told me the machine was made by Teckni-Craft out of Chicago for the Taylor Company. "They make all those soft-serve ice cream machines you see in McDonald's and Wendy's," she said.

I thanked her for her time and offered to buy her and her workmate a Slurpee. She just laughed and said, "We drink all those we can handle, but thanks anyway."

Art and I said goodbye to the clerk and began the long drive to Fort Worth.

I didn't talk much about the Slurpee machines as we drove, but my mind was working a mile a minute. I was writing in my notebook, trying to record everything I'd just seen and heard.

As Art approached the expressway taking us to Fort Worth, I asked if the airport was on the same road. When he said it was, I told him to drop me off. I knew there was a 9:00 p.m. departure to New Orleans that I'd taken once before and was anxious to return home.

At the passenger departure terminal, I told Art he might not hear from me tomorrow, but he could call at any time if he needed to talk. I was lucky there was an extra seat on the flight, and although I didn't arrive home until early in the morning, my mind was working through everything I'd learned about the Slurpee machines. New and exciting plans were bouncing around in my head, and I couldn't wait to share them with W.C.

SEVEN
Koolee is Born
"It would be an unbelievable money maker"

The 7-Eleven stores in Florida and other East Coast states were changing the ICEE brand to Slurpee, and I had no doubt it would remain just as popular with its new name. Fred Motalvo's Southern ICEE Beverage Corporation would retain control to some extent, but I was thinking beyond ICEE and the 7-Eleven stores.

On the flight back to Baton Rouge and throughout the weekend, I couldn't stop thinking about those Taylor machines in the Dallas store. It struck me that thousands of other convenience stores would love to have a frozen carbonated beverage machine of their own to compete with 7-Eleven. I knew of many financially secure independent convenience stores in Florida like Shop & Go, Lil General, Handy Foods, and Jiffy Foods.

This would be an incredible opportunity for the first person to approach them with a machine that made frozen drinks as good as the ICEE. The more I thought about it, the more determined I became to be that person.

Back home in Baton Rouge, I relished the hours spent with my family. The kids and I played in the park and had a great time reconnecting. I also had a long conversation with my partner, W.C. I filled him in on the 7-Eleven problem in Fort Worth and what I'd learned about the Taylor machines churning out Slurpees at the 7-Eleven store in Dallas. I also said I would give National ICEE my notice on Monday.

"Damn, are you sure you want to do that?" W.C. said. "That could make for a helluva mess for us."

"I don't think so," I replied. "I think Tom will be happy to see me leave. We got his new operations up and running, and he's making money with some good people at each of his locations. Tom isn't the kind of person who appreciates his operational workers to express different ideas or suggestions. All he wants around him are Yes Men."

W.C. wasn't saying much, but I knew he understood what I was saying.

"Besides," I continued, "our Salt Lake City franchise is booming, and I need to spend more time there working with Danny and our people. Salt Lake is doing good enough to support my salary. Is that okay with you, W.C.?"

He had no problem with that, and after briefly discussing my thoughts about moving forward, I hung up.

I gave Tom Devine my notice on Monday morning, and he didn't hesitate to accept it. I believe he was happy to be rid of me. I'd done an excellent job helping to get his company operations up and running, and he was receiving franchise fees from all of them, including ours in Salt Lake City. Of course, I never mentioned anything about the 7-Eleven Slurpee machines they were installing in Dallas or how Arthur and I had examined the Taylor machine and questioned the clerk about them.

I wasted no time following up on my plans and called the Taylor Machine plant in Chicago from the phone number I'd copied off the machine in Dallas. The national sales manager was happy to talk with me and said the Slurpee machine was a new product for them and their only customer was the 7-Eleven stores in Dallas.

That was good news, and I was encouraged to hear that they were open to discussing a deal for us to operate in Florida. He said I'd have to talk with Eddie Edwards, their distributor in Ft. Lauderdale, and he'd have him call me.

It didn't take long for the wheels to start turning. Eddie called within the hour and was excited to hear we wanted to buy three or four hundred machines. He suggested that if we signed a contract to purchase at least one hundred machines, he felt Taylor would give us exclusive rights for all of Florida. I hung up the phone, feeling like I'd hit the game-winning shot at the buzzer, and immediately called W.C.

My partner had always been a cautious businessman, and his first words were not *Congratulations, Bob, you hit it out of the park.* Instead, he said, "Can you get that many accounts in Florida?"

I assured him I could and rattled off all the contacts I'd made with Sav-A-Stop, like the Shop & Go stores in Tampa, Jiffy Food stores in Orange Park, and the Handy Food Stores. W.C. was familiar with all of them since they were his competitors, and I told him I'd already touched base with the owners, and they wanted to see me as soon as possible.

Now W.C. became excited. "Damn, Bob, four hundred machines would crank out a lot of drinks. If they produced just half of what each of our ICEE machines in Salt Lake are doing, it would be an unbelievable money maker."

I agreed and was happy to see he understood the advantages of expanding our partnership with the new business. Then he added, "But that's a lot of work. You'd have to hire workers and open offices. Are you up for that?"

The extra work needed to succeed would never be a problem for me. More importantly, was the chance to reunite with my family. "W.C.," I told him, "I want to come home to Florida, where most of my family and friends live. My kids are growing up, and I want time to help raise them. You know me, I'm not afraid to roll my sleeves up and work, so, yes, I'm ready and excited."

He understood perfectly what I was telling him, and we talked about our Florida operations. "I think Tampa is the right spot for our headquarters. I'll move my family there, so I'll be close to the main office and our biggest customers who are in the Tampa region—Shop & Go, Lil General, and Jiffy Food Stores."

I loved that Tampa had an international airport with excellent connections to every major city in Florida and throughout the country. Living in Baton Rouge had meant having to drive to New Orleans every week to catch a plane. Our phone conversation continued, and I told W.C., "I'm going back to Salt Lake this week and work with Danny. Next week we have an appointment with Eddie Edwards, but I think I can get him to fly into Pensacola. That's more convenient for both of us."

My oldest son Bucky, nine years old at the time, accompanied me to Salt Lake City. Being with Bucky kept me connected to the family, but I also put him to work assisting the route driver who delivered supplies to the store.

Danny, our Salt Lake City service manager, reported that our franchise had set a one-day national sales record for the number of ICEEs sold in one location—a total of 965 drinks in one day. As far as I know that record was never broken. We came close in some of our Koolee stores, like the first Shop & Go in Dade City that sold 843 in one day.

The following week I was back in Florida with W.C., and we met Eddie Edwards at the Pensacola airport. During our discussion, we learned the price of each machine was about $3,000, and the Taylor Machine company could only deliver ten machines a week at the time. Eddie said he'd need a few days to supply us with the first machines after we had placed the order and paid the deposit.

That timetable fit perfectly into my plans, and I told Eddie I'd be in touch as soon as we secured our agreements with the stores. I traveled to Tampa that night and met with the owners of Shop & Go and Little General stores the next day. I laid out the entire plan for them, although they already knew how the ICEE machines drove business in the 7-Eleven stores and wanted a piece of that action. Both of them gave me a letter of authorization to show Eddie Edwards and a list of their people who would handle the installations. The list included the locations of the stores to receive the first machines. While they waited for the ICEE dispensers, they would instruct their maintenance people to set up the electricity and water and run the syrup lines in their stores.

We picked the name Koolee for our new product, with the slogan "The drink that you eat!" Before I left, I told Mr. Jaeb of Shop & Go and Mr. Hornstra of Lil General Stores to prepare for a significant surge in business, telling them how well we were doing in Salt Lake City.

I drove back to Baton Rouge the next day, stopping first in Crestview to meet with W.C. to order the machines. He informed me he had travel plans. "I'm leaving Sunday for Africa on a mission trip for my church. Sorry, but this trip has been planned for months, so I need to go. We're building medical centers in some of the small villages near Johannesburg that badly need medical help."

I told him I'd miss him but thought I could handle the Koolee start-up. W.C. agreed. "You've organized all our operations anyway and I trust you to put the rest together. And we have enough cash to buy our first forty Koolee machines." He called in Jeff, his accountant, and instructed him to work with me on ordering the machines, sending me the money, and anything else I needed.

"Bob," W.C. said, "I'll be back in three weeks, maybe sooner. Good luck and don't spend all our money before I get back."

I informed Jeff that I'd use our Salt Lake ICEE franchise as a credit line for all the supplies, but I'd need a few checks for some of the necessary expenses. I planned to immediately lease a warehouse, purchase trucks, and order supplies.

Back in Tampa, I began my search for a warehouse to lease and a house to rent or buy quickly so I could move the family from Baton Rouge. I found a warehouse on Hillsborough Avenue in the same building with a hardware store and a large storage building in the back that had a high dock for loading and unloading delivery supplies. It was perfect. I immediately signed a lease for two years with yearly options.

Looking back, I'm amazed how everything fell into place so quickly. Lady Luck was certainly on my side, or maybe I had an angel sitting on my shoulder who couldn't wait to taste the new Koolee drink.

I found a house in Brandon, a friendly community part of the Tampa-St. Petersburg metropolitan area. The house was on Fig Tree Lane, just three blocks from the Nativity School and church. There was an open field behind the home where the neighborhood kids played, and it was only one block from the Brandon Swim Club. The house was for sale, and I bought it that day. The owner and I agreed on a monthly rental until closing. He said we could move in whenever we were ready. I called my wife to let her know I'd found the perfect house in Brandon. My next call was to Mayflower movers. Before the week was out, I'd leased a warehouse, bought a house, and registered the boys in their new school.

Once again, everything was falling into place, surely a sign the Koolee business would be successful. I thought about the lessons I learned from Pop. Never quit. Face your problems head-on. And take action as soon as possible. We may have been catching mullet or repairing an old jalopy at the time, but I never forgot his wise words. Fortunately, I was right. Koolee went on to be a successful business for me and W.C. and all our employees.

EIGHT
Expanding the Koolee Business
"We were always moving forward"

I followed the same procedures I learned while setting up the ICEE franchises out west to build our Koolee operations in Tampa, Orlando, Miami, Charlotte, N.C., Atlanta, Birmingham, and Chattanooga. There was no sense in reinventing the wheel, and I used the experience I gained with ICEE to find office and warehouse spaces and hire people in all those cities.

We started in Tampa and expanded from there. We were one of the first to sell Koolees and fountain drinks in promotional plastic cups. My son Danny and I started a separate company called Great Promotions to make collector cups. Popular cups included an Elvis Presley set and a set for the Miami Dolphins NFL team that went undefeated for their 16-game perfect season in 1972, then went on to win the Super Bowl. Great Promotions was hugely successful, and you can read more about that business in the next chapter.

We served over 2,500 convenience stores when I sold the Koolee Corporation in 1981 to Royal Cup in Birmingham, Alabama, and S & D Coffee in Charlotte, North Carolina. We had expanded the coffee services into the same stores, supplying them with coffee machines and supplies, and then did the same with fountain drink machines.

Our company created the first complete self-service counters in Florida for coffee, fountain drinks, and Koolees at the request of Robert Jaeb, the owner of Shop & Go. We made the counters and installed them with all the equipment in his existing stores. After that, Mr. Jaeb built all his new stores with self-service counters. Shop & Go started a trend that eventually spread through all the convenience stores in Florida.

While operating the Koolee Corporation, we started a concessions business and leased five of the Florida State Parks Concessions stands. These included Gold Head State Park in Clay County, Alafia River State Park in Hillsborough County, Manatee Springs State Park in Levy County, and Port St. Joe State Park. We opened one we called the Outpost.

My son Danny remembers how we got involved and how I had him working one of the concession stands through the first summer of his senior year in high school.

A WORD FROM MY SON DANNY

For about ten years before my dad sold the Koolee Corporation, we had branched out and were doing youth sports venues. At first, it was just Koolee machines, but then we got into the fountain drink business and popcorn and coffee. They lent themselves well to these events, and we did a lot of little leagues throughout Florida. Then dad bid on some of the state parks. They would want you to run the concessions and give them a percentage of the total revenue. We'd have to hire the personnel. Dad picked up four or five of them, including the one at Port St. Joe State Park. I had to go and stay about a month in the summer, hire someone, train him, and stock it with merchandise. All these state parks were a little different because they'd want things like aluminum foil and camping supplies, so we had to get into that aspect. When it was time to renew the five-year contract, we didn't bid on them because we were too spread out.

That was an interesting enterprise for us. I'm not sure we ever made any money in the concessions business, but we were always moving forward and trying new things.

My work ethic rubbed off on my children, who worked alongside me in our growing business portfolio. They may not have always been happy about it at the time, but as they look back on it now, they grin a lot. Even Kimmy helped when she got older.

GREAT PROMOTIONS

Great Promotions became the broker between the paper cup and plastic cup companies we were buying from and our Koolee business. The manufacturers were happy to buy from Great Promotions because we gave them all of the Koolee cup business, which, at the time, was one of the largest, if not the biggest, users of paper cups in the South.

I set Danny up in that business as a half owner. The plastic cup business was going so well that we ordered our own Kalizakie plastic injection machine from Japan and started manufacturing our own plastic cups. We soon found that one machine couldn't keep up with the demand, so we had to go straight to the plastic cup companies and broker for them. They bought our machine and contracted for our business.

We designed the first Baseball Cap cup and set up collector boards over our Koolee machines in all the stores. The promotion encouraged our customers to collect all the different teams until they had the entire collection of Major League Baseball teams' cap cups.

After that, we flew to California, met with Elvis Presley's manager, Colonel Tom Parker, and secured an agreement to produce an exclusive collection of Elvis cups. There were twenty cups with different photos of the "King of Rock' n' Roll." You can still find some of them selling on eBay.

Koolee sales were going through the roof. People loved the product, but they also wanted to collect whatever series of plastic cups we were selling at the time. As Elvis might have put it: We were rocking and rolling!

Later, Danny and I built the Park Place condominiums in Cedar Key. Park Place was a first-class destination for visitors with private balconies overlooking the Gulf of Mexico. Park Place was our first condo project. We sold it but still own two of the units.

We took the profits from that sale, bought some property on Cat Island near Yankeetown, and constructed a fishing camp for the family. We also purchased a small island in the same region we renamed Solano Island. In later chapters, you'll read more about our island experiences, including how we survived the No Name Storm of March 12, 2019.

NINE
Moving on with Life
"Family time was special"

Moving to Tampa with our new Koolee business gave me more precious family time. I was able to help my children with their after-school activities and local sports. They were all active kids, involved with Little League Baseball, county youth football, the county basketball league, and other activities.

We first joined the Brandon Little League, where I met George Nessmith and his wife, Tiny. They became two of my best friends in the world. We later moved to Riverview and signed up at East Bay Little League, where I coached for several years. All my children participated, including my daughter Kimberly. She played Tee-ball on my son Danny's team, who coached the Koolee Cats.

Here's a touching story about Danny and Kim when she played on his team. It's her turn at bat, and she says, "Uncle Danny, I can't go up to bat and let people see me with my hair all messed up."

He said, "Come over here, honey." He took her hat off, pushed her hair up, slipped the cap back on, and said, "Now you look great! Go up there and hit the ball hard off that stand. We need your help." She was so happy that her hair was fixed and went to bat wearing a big smile.

During our time there, I became president of East Bay Little League Baseball. Working with a great board of directors and all those kids was fun. At the same time, I coached in the Hillsborough County basketball league at the East Bay High School gym. Coaching with my son Britt, our team won the East

Bay League title and the Hillsborough County Championship several times in the playoffs. Our big man at center was Kenny Davis, an East Bay Little League star. Winning the championship made me feel like I was back in high school with my Fletcher teammates.

We played in the county youth football program during the fall and won the Hillsborough County championship in that league. One year at the county playoffs, my son David was the quarterback, and Brian was the center. Bo Cannon, my stepson, and Russell Frazer were our wide receivers.

My children were either playing or coaching a team. We were so involved in youth sports that sometimes we had two or three games in different leagues on the same day. Brian said he remembers when he played three games in one day—the last of the Little League Baseball season playoff games, a county basketball game at East Bay High, and soccer at the sports complex on Kings Avenue in Brandon. As they got older, they all played sports in high school. The guys played sports at their schools, and Kimberly became a cheerleader at her school.

A WORD FROM MY SON BRIAN

We were involved in East Bay baseball and East Bay basketball, and my dad coached a ton back then. He coached our basketball team. He coached our baseball team. He was an amazing coach, and frankly, if he had stuck with that, he could have been a college basketball coach. He was that good. One year he coached three teams of different ages. I was on the nine- and ten-year-old's team. My brother Dave was on the team that was eleven through twelve, and my brother Britt was on the thirteen through fifteen team—all in basketball. Each team dad coached won their division. And my brother Dave's team won the Hillsborough County basketball championship.

Dad also coached our nine to twelve Rag-Tag football team, all local kids from here in Riverview. I was nine and the starting center. Back then, the center was eligible as a receiver in Rag-Tag football. So, they would sneak me out now and then—I was a little rascal. In fact, my nickname was Big B because I was so small. But they would sneak me out for a pass after I hiked the ball. That nine through twelve-year-old' team, with my brother Dave and my stepbrother Bo on it, went all the way and won the county championship.

Despite all this activity and my work, we still found family time to go fishing in Cedar Key. Family time was special then because it included my Pop, who lived with us through the last ten years of his life. Pop moved from Jacksonville Beach to Tampa a year after my mother died in 1969. Grandma had died three years earlier, in 1966. We sold the old houses there, and the buyers tore them down and built new ones, but they left the chinaberry tree. Pop enjoyed living in the cottage on our Riverview property for the last ten years of his life.

Bobby with his family of young boys–from top left, Dan, Dave, Bo Cannon, Bucky front center, Brian in Bobby's lap, and Britt, right.

David Ray Solano was an amazing athlete.

All of the Solano boys were gifted athletes, including Brian, shown here playing Little League baseball.

POP'S OYSTER HARVEST

One of my fondest memories is a time when Pop and I were fishing in Cedar Key. He said, "Bubba, let's out in the back water and gather some oysters. Why should we pay $8.00 a bushel when we can get them here for free?"

Oyster and clam farming is big business in Cedar Key. Many fishermen took up clam farming after the state banned net fishing decades ago, including Danny and Britt, as you'll read about soon. Oysters have always grown naturally in the shallow coastal waters of the Gulf, and now the farmers grow them in floating cages near the clams. But they were still plentiful when Pop and I decided to harvest our own and save the $8.00 a bushel.

Of course, I agreed to take Pop, and since it was low tide, we could pluck the oysters from the inshore waters by hand. I slipped my little Jon boat into the water and waved at Pop telling him to climb aboard. He waded through the marshy water for only a few steps before getting stuck in the mud. He struggled to pull himself free but left one of the boots behind. I helped him into the boat, rescued the boot, and handed it to him.

Pop was still out of breath from marching through the mud to the boat, so I told him he could stay in the boat but asked him to clean the oysters I gathered and threw into the boat. He willingly cleaned them and tossed them in the tub.

I waded through the shallow water and pulled the flat-bottomed boat from one oyster bed to another. When we'd filled a number three washtub, I pulled the boat out of the water and carried the oysters to the fire pit. Pop stepped out of the boat, and became stuck in the mud again, losing both of his boots this time.

I thought about all the times we had hunted and fished together. Pop had always been in charge, but now it was my turn to lead. I dragged him out of the mud and helped him to a chair by our fire pit. Bless his heart, he was completely out of breath. After a while, he said, "Bubba, I will never for the rest of my life complain about the cost of oysters, no matter what they charge us."

We laughed and clinked our beer bottles together, toasting our oyster adventure. I built a fire, put a piece of tin over it, and laid the oysters on the tin to roast. We enjoyed our time together, and eating oysters today always brings me a smile. Pop is gone now, but he wouldn't believe that oysters cost $75 a bushel if he were still around. We loved having him with us because, to me, Pop was our family hero. He taught me many valuable lessons, which I passed along to my family. Whether we were repairing cars, casting our nets, or building my skeeter together, Pop knew the proper way to get things done. He worked hard and demonstrated through his approach to life that if you did your best and treated people fairly, everything would work out.

Thank you, Pop, for all your wonderful advice and the adventures we shared together. I'll never forget you and the family will never forget either. We love you forever.

TEN
The Beach Boy Becomes a USFL Owner
"Granted, it was expensive fun"

I sold the Koolee business in 1981, bought a boat, and went fishing. After two or three months of fishing every day, I'd had enough, so I purchased orange groves with some of the money from the Koolee sale. We bought around 440 acres of orange groves. My son Dan and I did most of the discing to keep the weeds and grass down. Along with weeds growing on the ground, orange growers face the continual problem of fighting vine weeds that can overcome a tree if you're not careful. We constantly pulled milkweed and possum grape vines out of the trees before they infested the entire tree.

Fortunately, I had a built-in labor force, and my boys earned their allowance by pulling vines. I also paid some of their school friends to help. Of course, my labor force wasn't always available during football and basketball season.

I also bought a jewelry business for my wife, Karen. I thought it was good to invest the money I was receiving from the sale of Koolee in hard assets.

Our entire family loved sports, and when the newly launched United States Football League (USFL). Based in Tampa, the league was created in 1982, and we wanted to be a part of it. John Bassett was the Tampa Bay Bandits franchise's majority owner, but they had several minority owners, including Hollywood star Burt Reynolds. I bought in as a limited partner. While the league only lasted three years, the Tampa Bay Bandits was successful, thanks to Coach Steve Spurrier's "Bandit Ball" offense.

My oldest boys, Danny and Britt, sometimes traveled with the team when they played the other USFL teams in major metropolitan areas like San Francisco, Los Angeles, Washington, D.C., Chicago, and Philadelphia. Britt has mixed reviews about our experience with the USFL.

A WORD ON THE TEAM FROM MY SON BRITT

I traveled a couple of times with the team and did sales calls in Philadelphia. I met a lot of the guys that were playing ball. I even tried out for the team myself. I was still in pretty good shape. But it all ended tragically. When the USFL folded, a couple of the people I was involved with committed suicide. They had stuck their necks out so far, and when Mr. Bassett died it left the league without good leadership. I guess the most interesting time was when I was in Philadelphia because the Philly fans are probably the worst in the world. The Bandits were playing Philadelphia, and there were a bunch of fights going on in the stadium. Beer is flying everywhere. It was bad.

Overall, my family and I had a lot of fun and exposure from the USFL investment. Granted, it was expensive fun—$500,000—but still fun.

You can tell from my work history that I'm always looking for new business opportunities, no matter what I'm involved with at the time. The USFL was no different. After becoming minority partners with the Tampa Bay Bandits, Danny and I flew to New York and acquired the rights to many USFL sports items, like caps, shirts, pins, and license plates. Great Promotions became fully involved in the sportswear business. We bought a large printing machine that could print eight T-shirts at a time and print logos on jackets, sweatshirts, and other team merchandise. We also contracted with suppliers for all the USFL and NFL caps.

Brian and I have constructed a small commercial park, which we build to suit our clients. One of our clients is the Bridgestone Corporation, the largest rubber company in the world and owners of the Firestone Tire stores.

We also built two condominium complexes in Steinhatchee, Florida, a picturesque little town in Florida's Big Bend region known for fishing and scalloping. The Sunset Place Resort has gorgeous views overlooking the Steinhatchee River, the Gulf, and the channel coming into the river. The complex faces west over the Gulf to catch the beautiful sunsets.

It hasn't been all work for the Solano family. As mentioned earlier, we bought a little slice of heaven and named it Solano Island. Our family gathered together on Solano Island for fishing and memorable reunions. And the island was also where I encountered what became known as the No Name Storm or sometimes called the Storm of the Century.

ELEVEN
Solano Island
"The lightning flashes helped illuminate the trail"

My family and I have had many adventures and experiences while fishing and camping together. We own a base woods camp on Cat Island near Yankeetown, Florida, a tiny coastal village about thirty minutes north of Crystal River. Known mainly as a commercial fishing village, Crystal River offers a wide range of fishing and scalloping opportunities. If visitors would rather relax, they can lay back and watch flocks of egrets feeding along the waterways.

The sleepy little town's main claim to fame happened in 1961 when Elvis Presley and a Hollywood film crew arrived to film part of Elvis's ninth movie, *Follow That Dream*. We weren't there to see Elvis, but we followed our dream when we built a fishing camp on nearby Cat Island.

You can only access the island by a bridge we built and named the *Number One Bridge*. We also own an island of about fifteen acres on the Gulf just off the coast of Gulf Hammock in the same area. We usually visit what we call "Solano Island" by airboat or put our boats in at the Yankeetown Marina. Tooke Creek encircles the island on three sides, and marshes cover the rest of the island.

You'll frequently find us fishing and camping on the island. After cleaning our catch, Britt and I fry them up with grits or French fries, the same way the Solano family has done for years while living and enjoying Florida's natural resources, first along the St. Augustine coast and now on the Gulf side. When we're together during these hunting and fishing outings, I feel the strong family bonds I formed growing up with Pop. He taught me the Minorcan lifestyle, passed on through the generations from one family to another. I've kept these traditions alive, passing the cultural torch to my children and grandchildren.

STORM OF THE CENTURY

One memorable adventure occurred several years ago when my son Dan, my good friend Brian Clements, and I were fishing off the island in the creek. It didn't take an expert outdoorsman to notice the sky over the Gulf turning black, telling us a storm was on the way. We quickly gathered our gear and returned to the airboat to make a run back to the Marina. The airboat had other ideas and refused to start. We worked on it for over an hour but to no avail. By now, the sky had turned even blacker, and a steady wind whipped through the trees. Then we were engulfed by heavy rain with rumbles of thunder and sheets of lightning in the distance.

We had two choices: either hunker down where we were without shelter from the approaching storm or make our way through the marshy woods toward our base camp some five miles away. We agreed we needed to move, and we set out on foot with no flashlights, one machete, and a cooler full of fish we refused to leave behind. We first pulled the boat up as high as possible and tied it down. By then, the rain and wind had kicked up several notches, lashing our faces and soaking our clothes. The black clouds had transformed the afternoon sky into a nighttime setting, though I hoped we had enough daylight left to help us navigate the hammock. But it quickly became so dark we were tripping over tree roots.

Mother Nature had dumped a massive storm on us. Blasts of thunder and frightening lightning strikes accompanied the wind and rain. But the lightning flashes helped illuminate the trail and set our course through the swamp. In the dark, we couldn't see our hand in front of our face and had to wait for the next flash to get our bearings and move on.

Soon we found ourselves wading through waist-deep water, but we knew our camp was close to the creek. We were not exactly sure where we were until we came to the wire fence that ran north and south, separating the hammock land from the state-owned land. Feelings of relief swept over us because we knew the wire fence ran right by our Cat Island base camp, and we could follow it south to the camp. In the dark and slashing rain, I kept a hand on the fence to be sure we didn't drift off course.

Along the way, we jumped over a gator and a couple of snakes lying on the higher banks. I'm not sure who was scared the most—the gators and snakes or us. We finally made it to Spring Run Creek adjoining our base camp, and you never saw three happier, wet, and cold men. We stopped and rested for a few minutes before crossing the swollen creek, which was now about waist high. Fortunately, the creek had a hard pan bottom, and we had plenty of enthusiasm now because the camp was within sight.

I'll let Dan take over at this point and relate his memory of this incident.

A WORD FROM DANNY

We were walking in water up to our waist because the storm had pushed in with a six-foot storm surge. We had to wade through hammocks and open marsh where gators and snakes were, but we had no other choice. We could climb a tree and stay up there all night or keep walking and hope we found the camp. We kept walking and found the fence. Dad and I knew the fence line and followed it to the camp in four feet of water. We didn't own the camp at the time. It belonged to a friend and was the last camp before you reached the water. He had one of these old doors with jalousie windows, little three-inch panes, maybe twelve inches long. So, I slid out one of the panes to get my hand inside and unlock the door. We were soaked and freezing, but we needed to get inside because we knew he had a phone.

Inside, I immediately built a fire in the pot belly stove. The three of us huddled around the fire, dog-tired, dirty, and soaked to the skin. We looked at one another and broke out laughing with joy, knowing we'd lived through a crazy adventure we'd be talking about for years. We didn't know it then, but we'd survived what the locals would call "the storm of the century." It had blown in from the Gulf, catching most people by surprise.

We were safe, but we still needed to get off the island. Dan adds another piece to this story.

We got inside and tried to reach my brother Britt. We were lucky he was at the cottage in Riverview, but he didn't have a phone there, so we called my wife, and she went over and got Britt.

I knew my son Britt would find a way to save us through hell and high water. When we explained the situation, Britt didn't hesitate. He said, "I'm on my way."

Britt lived in Tampa, about a three-hour drive from Cat Island. I told Dan and Brian that help was on the way, and we could relax for a spell. It was already about midnight, and we enjoyed the cabin's warmth for the next two hours before buttoning up the rain gear we'd left behind in the camp and preparing to hike out to meet Britt at the Number One Bridge.

Trudging slowly through knee-deep water that now covered the entire island, we occasionally stepped into deep holes that dotted the trail to the bridge. Britt arrived about the same time we did, and we were glad to see him. We piled into his Jeep, and Britt motored out through rising tidal water from the Gulf and rain washing over the saturated roadway. The water nearly reached the jeep's headlights, but Britt eased through it so slowly that he was barely moving. He stopped when he felt the front end going down, backed up, and maneuvered around the holes. He did a hell of a job getting us out of that flood without flooding his SUV.

BRITT'S SIDE OF THE ADVENTURE

I got a call late at night, about 10 or 11 o'clock. I was in Riverview, and they were up in Inglis. I didn't realize how bad the weather was, but I had my Jeep and thought I could get the guys out of there. As I neared where I was going to meet them, the water was almost waist deep in some places, and I couldn't get all the way back to them. It was bad—raining, storming, the wind blowing like crazy. The water was up to my door, and I couldn't get back to them. I was leaning out the window with one of those million-watt candle power things you plug into your vehicle, trying to make sure I didn't get off that road because there were deep ditches on both sides. And I couldn't see anything except where my headlights were, and sometimes the Jeep's lights were submerged. It was pretty serious. I drove back as far as I could go and stopped and listened, but I couldn't hear anything. I beeped my horn a couple of times, and still nothing. I sat there for about ten minutes. I wasn't about to get out and wade through waist-deep water to find those guys. I told them they had to meet me. Besides, I had no clue exactly where I was at the time. I knew I was close but wasn't sure. Finally, I saw a light in the distance and started beeping the horn again. Sure enough, here comes three guys dragging a cooler with mud in it. I told them to throw that thing out. I think we got back about four or five in the morning.

After the storm passed, we returned to the island and retrieved the airboat. We had to pull it back to the Yankeetown boat ramp, load it up, and take it to a mechanic. That was one hell of an adventure worthy of a separate book. It all worked out for us, but I later heard that two people were killed in Keaton Beach, near Perry, Florida.

TWELVE

An Airboat Adventure with Brian
"There's a good story about life right there"

Another time, Brian and I were fishing at the bend of Spring Run Creek by our base camp, and we hit a submerged rock that knocked a hole in the airboat. Luckily, the hole was on the side of the boat and not the bottom. Airboats are flat-bottomed crafts propelled by an aircraft-type propeller. Because they don't have a submerged propeller, you can run them over shallow swamps, marshes, and even mudflats with only an inch of water. I've even run them over wet ground.

But a hole in the boat was a problem. We were five or six miles from the boat ramp, and sunset was only a few hours away. We planned to run the boat toward the landing until we took on too much water to keep running. Then we'd have to pull her out on the marsh or a mudflat and let the water drain. The rising water in the boat forced us to stop by the time we reached the creek leading to the landing. I spotted a mudflat in the middle of the creek and pulled up on it. While waiting for the water to drain, we sat drinking beer, knowing we'd be back on dry land in no time since the boat ramp was only a half-mile away.

Suddenly, the biggest wild gator I ever saw swam out of the marsh across from where we were sitting. The critter stared at us with hungry eyes like he'd found himself a good meal and slipped into the creek about ten feet from us. I turned to Brian and said, "This damn boat has drained enough. Empty or not, we're leaving."

We jumped into the airboat, sloshing through the water covering our an-kles, cranked her up, and raced toward the landing. We held our breath and said a little prayer as we watched the water fill the boat. Good fortune was on our side that day because we made it within fifty feet of the landing before the airboat sank. Thank God we were now in only three feet of water. We slipped over the side, pulled the boat to the edge of the creek, and tied her to a tree. We retrieved our cooler of fish and waded to the landing.

An older man fishing off the bank had been observing the entire scene. As we approached, he shook his head and said, "That's why I don't own a boat. Too damn much trouble. Look at it now, all sunk and damaged."

"Yes, sir," I said, "there's a lot of truth to that. How's your fishing going?"

"Not a damn bite, except for a little catfish," he said.

When we got to the truck, I pointed back to the fisherman and said to Brian, "There's a good story about life right there."

Brian looked puzzled and asked, "What do you mean, dad?"

"In life you can stand on the bank and not catch any fish while watching opportunities pass you by. Or you can take the chance of getting in a boat and going after the fish and maybe catching a cooler full of them. The same applies to life. Don't stand around worrying about what might happen. Take some chances and take advantage of the opportunities that come your way."

These Solano Island stories are only a few of the adventures I've had with my family and friends. I could share more, but there's not enough time or pag-es to tell them all. In between the time we spent fishing and hunting, we kept working. Brian and I are currently remodeling the Surfside Cottages located on Vilano Beach in St. Augustine. My daughter Kimberly's husband Steven can repair almost anything. They're both helping with the renovations. This property has had a special place in our family history for many years.

**An airboat adventure with Brian, Mathew and
Bobby, waving in the background.**

KIM'S STORY

Dad acquired the Vilano Beach property almost fifty years ago. He used to party there when he was a kid running up and down north beach. He used to hang out at this piece of property and build bonfires and take girls out there. The owner would come running with a shotgun and chase daddy off, yelling, "Bobby Solano, you're never going to amount to anything."

He pulled in there one day and knocked on the man's door. When the guy came out, he asked him, "Do you remember me?" the man said, "Bobby Solano, am I going to have to run you out of here?" They laughed and walked across the street to the beach together. While walking on the beach, dad told him how he'd started the Koolee Company, and he had all these kids, and we all lived in Tampa. The old man was happy to hear how well he was doing.

Daddy told me this story long ago, and it always resonated in my mind. He said that when he was talking with the old man, a dune buggy came by, made a circle, and stopped. Daddy said he could see a huge school of mullet right off the shore, and the guy grabbed his cast net, threw it, and pulled in a load of mullet. Dad said he turned, looked at the old guy, and said, "I'd like to buy this property. Would you sell it to me?"

And the guy said, "Absolutely!"

Dad bought the property, and there were these old army barracks on the property they rented. We fixed them up like bed and breakfasts with towels, linens, and big screen TVs on the wall. They had full kitchens with pots, pans, silverware, plates, and grilling utensils. They fell apart over the last three-and-a-half years, and the stress of the upkeep almost moved dad to sell them. But we have a lifetime of memories on that beach, so we talked dad out of selling, and we're fixing them up.

I'm so proud of my daughter. Kimberly has a real estate broker license, owns Solano Real Estate, and has the support and help of her son Rene, who owns a successful roofing business.

I feel blessed to have a family so loaded with talent. I'm proud of all my children and how they've carved their own paths in life. The whole family is self-sustaining in their own businesses.

The Solano family's Surfside Cottage in Vilano Beach.

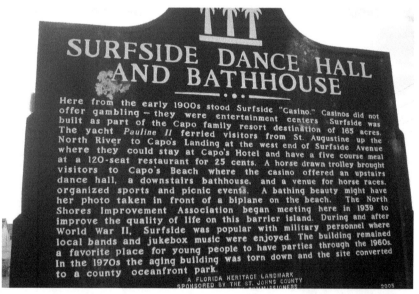

Historical marker describing the Surfside Casino where Bobby and his friends danced the night away on weekends.

THIRTEEN
My Life in Rotary

For over one hundred years, Rotary International has brought people together from across the globe to take action and solve problems. The fellowship at the community level is wonderful, but more importantly, the 46,000 Rotary Clubs have worked together to fight polio, promote peace, provide clean water and sanitation, help mothers and children, and much more.

Rotary has been an important part of my life for forty-one years. I'm proud of my Brandon Rotary Club and what we've accomplished working together. I was honored to be the club's Legacy Award winner in 2018 and recognized for perfect attendance and service to the club. What follows is my response to that honor.

It's been my pleasure to be a member of the Brandon Rotary Club for almost forty years. I was introduced to Rotary by a truly great friend, Mr. Charlie Burnett, who was president of the club at the time. I promised Charlie I'd try to be a good Rotarian member, but I was so busy I couldn't be part of the club's leadership. I said, "Charlie, I am president of three or four corporations and president of the East Bay Little League, where all my kids are involved. I don't have time for anything else."

He said, "Bob, that's exactly what we need. We want loyal, good members first. The club will take care of itself."

I remember Charlie sitting outside the clubhouse at Tiger Lake for our annual fishing trip each year, welcoming everybody as they arrived. In those days, we caught, cleaned, and cooked all the game at our wild game cookout every year. For years we held it at George Simmons ranch in Riverview. George was another great Rotary member. We would take a day off and cut palms for wild palm cabbage stew.

My son Brian joined the club and has been an active member, along with Danny and my daughter Kimberly. Danny and Brian are Paul Harris Fellows, and Kimberly will be one soon.

The Brandon Rotary Club has been a leader in our community, aggressively pursuing solutions to area problems. Along with supporting multiple charities, we purchased and developed land here in Brandon, where we created the Rotary Camp of Florida, serving sick and disabled children. Today, many of the other Florida Rotary Clubs are supporting the camp.

THANK YOU, MEMBERS OF BRANDON ROTARY, FOR LETTING ME BE A PART OF THIS CLUB. GOD BLESS.

The Solano family was all there when Bobby was honored with the Rotary Legacy Award at the 2018 annual dinner. Left to right: Brian, Bobby, Britt, David, Dan, his wife Patty, and Kimberly.

The Rotary Motto
Service Above Self

PART FIVE

The Solano Family

Bobby's Rules to Live by:

11. It's never too late to be happy but <u>remember</u> it's all up to you.

12. Whatever doesn't kill you truly does make you stronger.

13. When in doubt just take the next small step.

ONE
The Chinaberry Tree
"It was still standing tall and green"

I wanted Brian, Britt, Daniel, and Kimberly to share some of their memories and experiences as part of the Solano family. But before they contribute their memories, allow me to look back again and share a story of a recent visit I made to my old homestead. You've already read about my childhood in Adamsville and how we lived in the woods, not far from what we referred to as "the rich folks" in Ponte Vedra Beach.

Our house was on a dirt road named Theodore Street, and the only houses on that street belonged to my family. I can still picture my grandmother working in her garden, planting flowers and vegetables and lining the fence with rose bushes. About the time I was born in 1935, someone gave her a small Chinaberry tree, and she planted it in the front yard.

The tree was only four or five feet tall when I was waddling around the yard. Later, as we both grew taller, I knocked one of its limbs off playing basketball and was rewarded with a whipping. Grandma made it known that her Chinaberry tree was off limits to everybody, and Pop punished me whenever I climbed Grandma's tree.

That was a long time ago, and nearly everything has changed. Adamsville is gone, along with the scrublands and fields where I played. In its place is a new residential community called The Sanctuary. One day, Brian and I were in Vilano Beach working on the Surfside Cottages, and I said, "Let's drive to

Jacksonville Beach, and I'll show you where I used to live."

We found Theodore Street, and everything was different, but the China-berry tree in the front yard of a lovely home was still there. The old tree had suffered from years of wear and storm damage, not to mention what I had in-flicted on it, but it was still standing tall and green with plenty of Chinaberries on it. Brian and I stared at the tree from our pick-up, and I told him stories that he'd heard more than once. Then we climbed out of the truck, and I knocked on the front door of the house. A young lady came out, and I explained that I grew up on the exact spot where she now lived. I asked her if we could take a picture of the Chinaberry tree. Of course, she agreed and took our picture in front of the old Chinaberry tree.

I've had a rich and adventurous childhood but seeing that Chinaberry tree reminded me you couldn't go home again. All the trees are gone from the Adamsville of my youth. The endless fields of green palmetto scrubs are gone. The sprawling oak hammock where I hunted squirrels almost every Saturday morning is gone.

Gone is driving on the beach from the St. Johns Jetties in Atlantic Beach to Matanzas Inlet on Vilano Beach, where we fished and searched for turtle eggs. Gone are most of the beautiful sand dunes that once lined the coast, replaced by houses and more houses. Condos and more condos.

I suppose people my age spend more time thinking about the past, so being lost in nostalgia is to be expected. But I wouldn't have written this book if I hadn't remembered those days filled with adventure and achievement.

Looking back on my life's journey and where I am today, I still have to say my family is my proudest achievement. I want my three sons and my daughter to share some of their memories and personal achievements with you. Brian, Britt, Dan, and later Kimberly helped me in my various business enterprises while establishing their own careers. We'll start with my youngest son, Brian Solano.

**Bobby and Brian pose in front of the old Chinaberry tree that was
planted in the front yard of their Adamsville home.**

TWO
Brian Solano's Story

Some of my earliest memories growing up in Riverview are around a pond where we fished. We would cast a net and catch bream and bass. We're also on a river, and growing up here, I thought it was normal to be like Huckleberry Finn. We'd walk along the riverbanks when the tide was low, and we'd have mud all over us. We used to catch flounder in our hands back in the day.

But it wasn't all play. When dad owned the Koolee Corporation, he built a 12,000- square foot warehouse here in 1973 on some property that we still own today. During the summers, we would work in the warehouse assembling coffee kits for the stores. The kits contained filter packs of coffee with stirrers and sugar. We packed them in a box, taped them up, and labeled them. We did that as kids, but frankly, I think it was more stressful for dad and my brother Dan working with him in the office than for us. While they worked in the office, we'd play, making forts with the boxes. We started with good focus and got a lot of work done, but it was quite a chore to keep that going. I probably did that from ages nine through twelve.

Later, I tried to play pro baseball and had a few injuries. I had shoulder surgery at the University of Florida. When I was rehabbing, I moved back home and went to a local community college to walk on the team. It was going well, but my shoulder never really came back. I was at a student government meeting one day, and a lady who also worked for an advertising agency came up to me and asked if I'd ever thought about getting into modeling. I told her

I hadn't thought about modeling, but I'd dated a girl in high school who was involved in the business.

I was always active in sports, but I wasn't sure where baseball was going, so I called that lady and went to their office. They made an appointment with a photographer for my headshots, and before I knew it, my modeling career took off. The next thing I knew, I was living all over the world. I was involved in the modeling industry for about fifteen to eighteen years. I did a lot of acting as well. I've got six years invested in the Screen Actors Guild union from doing commercials.

When I was twenty-three, I was in a jeep accident and fractured a cervical vertebra, that slowed me down. But I got back into it and became bigger than ever in that industry. I ended up living in Italy, Paris, and New York and worked for the world's most prominent designers, from Giorgio Armani to Calvin Klein. I was very blessed. But I reinjured my neck, and started working out and doing yoga.

Dad called me one day and said, "Son, if you're ever going to get out of that business, I'd love to have you work with me on some of our real estate ventures."

I was in my mid-thirties, and had a chance to help my dad, help the family, and start a new career. I returned home and interviewed with him, did some work, and went back. I was living in Chicago, and took some time to consider his offer, did more yoga, and eventually made the decision. I've been here for twenty-one years working alongside my dad.

The tales of my modeling career still echo around our family. One night, while we were sitting at the dinner table, my nephew David said to me, "Uncle Brian, you were really big in that modeling business. Why are you back here working with Poppa now?"

My nephew David has a great sense of humor, always has and still does. I said to David, "You know it was really, really stressful. I was doing a lot of runway shows, and all the female models were getting dressed backstage with us and running around with hardly anything on. I couldn't handle that stress anymore, and I'd rather be down here working with Poppa than doing that."

David looked at me like I'd just stepped off a flying saucer and said, "Uncle Brian, did a boulder fall on your head?"

One of the things I got involved with initially when I went to work with dad was building a 12,000-square foot warehouse for a "Build-to-Suit" tenant. We called it Business Park at Palm River Road. I acted as the general contractor, and in recent years we built another building on that property for that same tenant and another tenant. During those years, I helped when he was completing a project in Steinhatchee, and then he and I were involved in building a condo complex there called Steinhatchee Place. Steinhatchee is a good four hours from our office in Riverview, so it involved a lot of driving. My dad and I did most of that together, but there were times when we had to go separately. But we work well together, and we enjoy the process.

He also found a beautiful piece of property right at the mouth of the river and began building a complex called Sunset Place. We were blessed to sell out all the condo units in that complex.

Most recently, we've been working on renovating the Vilano Beach cottages built in the 50s. They need a lot of love to restore them. We worked on that ourselves or with family members and maintenance men doing some simple remodeling, but we'll use a general contractor for most of the work going forward.

We have space for another building on the Palm River property, but this will be the last one for the time being. My father and I have worked hard for years, so we're trying to get to a point we can work at a much slower pace and enjoy fishing with family.

I have nothing but respect and admiration for my father and how far he rose from his childhood. What he learned from his upbringing was self-reliance. You learn some incredible traits when you go out twenty miles in the woods to hunt or drive up the beach searching for fish. For example, going hunting twenty miles in the woods back then, there were no convenience stores. There were no cell phones. You better know how to repair everything on that truck or beach buggy. You better have everything you need to fix a tire or whatever to get back with your catch or kill so you can eat. It made him very thorough with his analysis of what you've got to do before you go out. And I think that carried into his life, that process of how you had to be thorough, and you had to be aggressive to survive. Because if you didn't have something you needed to fix whatever's broken or didn't have enough gas, then you had to walk twenty miles back.

Anybody can be talented or have the ability to be a great salesman or athlete, but if you don't have the discipline, you can't continue to be a success. Hard work, discipline, and the patience to persevere are the best qualities I learned from my father.

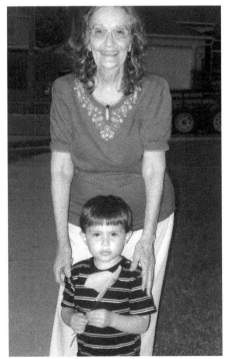

Young Brian with his mother Diane at Disney on Ice.

Brian enjoyed success as a male model, traveling the globe during his career.

THREE
Britt Solano's Story

I'm the middle of five boys. Our oldest brother Bucky was killed water skiing. We were still living with our mom in Jacksonville at the time—myself, Dave, and Brian, but Bucky had decided to move in with dad in Riverview. Bucky and a couple of his buddies were water skiing, and apparently, an old tug came by, and he wasn't paying attention and skied into a dock. It knocked him out. He wasn't wearing a life vest since you weren't required to wear one back then, and he sank to the bottom of the river. They got my dad, brought him back to the dock, and dad dove for him until he found him. I don't know how many times he dove for him. That was a terrible tragedy for the entire family.

About a year or so later, I moved in with my dad. I was eleven and in the sixth grade. My brothers and I had our spats like all of us do, but we stood up for each other and were pretty darn close. We all played sports and were extremely competitive.

Poppa Pete lived with us for the last ten years of his life in a little cottage on our Riverview property. His name was Bartola Edward Pacetti. I'm Bartola Solano. He was a great guy. He was the one who taught me to throw a cast net when I was about six. I forgot to let go of the weight, and my two front teeth came out. But they were coming out anyway. Poppa Pete was mechanically inclined and loved to fish.

I learned so much from him. I remember staying with him when my parents went away, and Poppa Pete and I stayed behind. We would crab and fish, cook dinner and hang out. He was a great guy to hang out with. He always had a beer in his hand. I don't remember him driving without a beer. I swear to God.

I was too young to help when dad had his Thrifty Discount Stores. That was mostly Bucky and Dan. And speaking of being young, my given name is Bartola, named after Pop, but I soon acquired the nickname of Britt, and when I was young, they sometimes called me "Britt the Brat."

It wasn't until dad had the Koolee business that I got involved. I worked in that business in one form or another for most of my life. We started out working for a dollar a day, and we played more than we did anything. That was when we were real young, but as we got older, we worked in the warehouse. Later, I was on the road delivering all over the southeast. I remember driving to Miami and leaving at four in the morning. I dropped the supplies off at a warehouse in Miami, turned around, and drove back the same day. I remember going to Atlanta with my brother. We drove through the night to get there. I had to load up trucks the next morning. I was about seventeen at the time.

I worked hard. It wasn't a question of whether I do it or not, but "What do we have to do?" I can tell you one thing: As I grew up, I would do things as far as workwise, and I wouldn't think twice about it. Other people might look at it and say, "I ain't doing that." I just assumed that's what we all did. I remember cleaning out sewers and getting my hands in it and didn't think nothing of it. I just did it because it needed to be done.

I played football and baseball in college. I weighed about 230, 6'2", and was in good shape. I ended up being a tight end and getting up to about 245. Back then, 245-250 was a big guy on the field. I lettered in baseball, and then I got in a whole bunch of trouble one summer doing some stupid things kids do. It was about two years before I returned to college. But I went back to get an education instead of just playing ball. That was a different avenue that I took, and it was a good one.

I was a theater major and did thirty or forty plays, acting in them, working backstage, and even directed one. After I graduated from college, I was still doing my master's work. They paid me to go to school, but I was burnt out. My brother Brian was modeling, and I thought I get to go to Europe, get paid, and hang out with the most beautiful women? I'm in!

Now Brian was a real model. I'm a rough, rugged kind of guy. Brian was more of a pretty boy and had a better attitude for that job. I didn't have a good attitude. I wanted to work, but other people had total control over whether I worked or not, and it had nothing to do with me. Brian traveled all over the world. He had a pretty smile, a young, pretty boy. And as I said, I was a rough-cut dude. But I was ripped.

I did that back and forth for a couple of years all over Europe until one day, I was sitting in Manhattan in Times Square in a tiny efficiency costing us about $2,000 a month. I had been working with Ralph Lauren twice a month, which would pay the bills because I was getting paid like two grand a day. I was trying to get other jobs. You know how it is—starving actors and artists. Then the Ralph Lauren jobs stopped coming, and I was working in a warehouse. So, I was sitting in Manhattan basically broke, and decided I wasn't raised this way. I don't want to live this way. I came back to Florida, got my captain's license, started working with my brother, and from then on, I was pretty much on the water.

Now I'm involved with clam farming. It began about 1996, after I'd just returned from Europe and saw that Dan was involved in the aquaculture business. I did a little part-time work for him, so I worked for my brother for about four years doing everything from sales to running routes to farming and diving because I used to love to dive. I would do a lot of diving, plating clams, pulling clams, stuff like that. In '99, we had a bad El Nino that caused a lot of freshwater encroachment that killed a large percentage of the clams up here. He had to shut his facility down south and move everything to Cedar Key. At the same time, I wanted to move to Cedar Key. Then about 2000, dad said he'd loan me money to start my own business clamming in Cedar Key. And that's how I got started farming. I guess it took me about ten years to pay him off. But Dan does the selling. I'm a farmer.

My father had an intense desire to succeed. Here's a story I heard from my Aunt Joyce about when they were kids, and they'd go to the beach. They'd walk over to the Ponte Vedra Club, which was all fenced off with a pool behind the fence. The pool was strictly for club members, and only the rich folks were members. They would go up there when they were little kids, lean on the fence and look at the wealthy people. The two of them swore at the time that they would be rich enough to be a member there. I think they decided they would work their way out of poverty and find a way to get rich. And they did.

What did I learn from my dad? There's a lot. One thing is not being afraid to work hard. I've never been scared of anything, and I don't know if I learned that from him or not. I was the middle of five boys, so I was the one who went out in the dark when everyone else wouldn't. I learned a lot about sports from my dad. He taught me that if you want to achieve, you have to put in the extra ten percent that nobody else will do. No matter what you do in this life, if you want to succeed and be better than anybody else, you must put in the extra work.

That's what I learned from my dad.

The Solano men together during a Rotary wild game cookout in the early 90s. From left, Britt, Dave, Bobby, Brian, and Dan.

Britt Solano and his son, "Jakey" – Jacob – reeled in big ones in the Southern KingfishTournament in Charleston, South Carolina. Jacob took third place in the Junior Division.

FOUR
Daniel Solano's Story

It's true that dad put us to work at an early age, but it was all part of supporting the family. I first helped at dad's Thrifty Discount Stores—stocking shelves and pricing. That was when you had to put a sticker on every item. I was about eight to ten when I was doing that stuff, and I enjoyed it. I was about twelve when we moved to Tampa, and he had the Koolee business. As soon as I could, I began working with dad. When I turned fifteen, I applied for a program where they'd let you out of school early if you had a job, and you'd get two elective credits if you maintained that job. My dad's warehouse wasn't too far from where we lived, and I worked in the warehouse.

I've told my kids that it took me three years to make it to the air conditioning. My first job was working in the warehouse unloading trucks, and it was hot. It took me three years to make it to the office—the air conditioning. If you were playing baseball or other sports, you wouldn't have to work in the warehouse on Saturdays because of your games. But when the season was over, there was no sitting home on Saturdays and watching cartoons. You either worked in the yard, or you worked in the office.

It was teaching everybody a work ethic. That's how my dad started. He wasn't trying to teach us something that he didn't know. He worked his butt off to make it in life. He'll tell you his first summer job was digging ditches. Before they had the equipment to do that, people had to dig them with shovels. He told me, "I was usually the only white person in that group. But you know what, I worked hard, and got to be second best at it. There was only one guy I couldn't beat."

That was part of my dad's philosophy of life. He learned how to enjoy that work—make a game out of it, make a challenge out of it. Something other than the drudgery of knowing you would go to work and dig a hole for eight hours. I used to listen to him tell those stories, and it made sense to me. It's an opportunity. It's not something you hate doing. You turn it into something positive. I'll never forget that.

I was the businessman in our family. I owned my first business when I was 17 with my dad when we started the Great Promotions company. I went to college for about six months, but didn't stay. Great Promotions was a plastic cup manufacturing business. We used paper cups for the Koolees, and a promotion company showed us a plastic cup using major league baseball logos. We tried them, and they did well. People liked to collect the cups and reuse them. We were selling so many we decided to make our own and bought a machine to manufacture the cups. We had a lot of business right off the bat, and when we showed the cups to a couple of our big convenience store chains, they liked the idea. We extended the line of cups and added collector's cups featuring everything from Star Wars characters to Elvis.

I'm not sure what happened after that since I went away to college, but we did a lot of business and manufactured a lot of cups. That was about the time my dad sold Koolee. We used that money to build a condominium project here in Cedar Key in the early 80s. When I was about 22 or 23, we built a 36-unit condominium here and kept a couple of them after we sold the others.

After that, I worked with the Jaeb family, who owned the Shop & Go chain. They wanted to be developers, so I was helping them with some property they'd bought. They asked me to come to work for them, and I ran their real estate business for five or six years until we developed what needed to be developed, sold what needed to be sold, and then got out of the business. Then I started growing clams, which I've been doing for the last thirty years in Cedar

Key.

My dad had been to Cedar Key when he was a young man hunting and fishing. He had a cousin who lived in Trenton, a small town about 50 miles from Cedar Key.

My dad would visit his cousin, and they'd go hunting. Then they'd go over to Cedar Key to go fishing. When I was about 16, I was working for Koolee, running what they called vacation routes. When guys would go on vacation, I'd run their routes. I had been working around Cedar Key for two weeks, and my dad said, "Check around and see if there's any real estate there. When I was a kid, I used to fish there, and maybe we can get a little place to go fishing."

I picked up some real estate flyers and brought them back to him. Ultimately, he found a little house on the water and bought it. That was in the mid-70s. On weekends we'd come up from time to time to fish. And then, in the early 80s, we came up here and saw that somebody was starting a little condominium project. I bought one of the units. They were only about thirty thousand dollars back then. I thought, "Hey, why don't we see if we can buy some land and build one, too?" We looked around and found the property and built those condos. But they were small, more like a motel, 600 square foot, and 1,000 square foot units. We used the money from the plastic cup business for that successful project.

In 1990, I'd just gotten divorced from my first wife after twelve years of marriage. We didn't have any children. I was about thirty-two and wanted a change from having to wear a shirt, tie, and slacks every day. I was in real estate, and you had to dress that way, but I was getting tired of that and was hoping to do something different in life. I started coming to Cedar Key to relax, and they'd just had a situation where they closed a section for oystering because the waters had become polluted. The state had also imposed a net ban, and many commercial fishermen and oystermen were out of work. The state launched a program to train the oystermen and commercial fishermen to grow clams and gave them seeds and bottomland to farm. Ricky Cook, dad's good friend, went through this program. He was gung-ho, but he didn't have any money. The truth was that nobody in that program had any money. The state was going to give them a few seeds, pat them on the back, and say, "Good luck."

Ricky came to us and suggested doing a joint venture. He said he could buy the seed and grow the clams and sell them, and we could split the revenue. We said sure, let's try it. I got interested in it while doing real estate, and after working with Ricky for a year or two on that joint venture, I decided I wanted to go after it. Ricky wanted to stay small, and dad wasn't interested in growing the business either. I approached Stephen Jaeb from the convenience store family, and we became partners. Stephen and I were the same age and grew up together. Our parents did business together for a long time, so we knew each other well. Both of our companies sold in about the same three- or four-year time frame—Shop & Go and Koolee. Of course, they got a lot more for their business, about $170 million, which was a hell of a lot of money in the mid-eighties. They had 450 stores, all in Florida and South Georgia.

After that joint venture with Ricky, Stephen and I put up some serious money, bought some land, and started the business. My company, Cedar Key Aquaculture Farms, sold four million dollars worth of clams last year. Our biggest customer is Costco. We've been doing business with them for about twenty years. I began by selling to smaller seafood companies, mainly in the northeast because that's where the biggest volume is, but about a third of them screwed us. After that, I had a conversation with myself. I said, "Dan, you need to find a customer that wants to be loyal."

That led to us chasing retailers. We were doing business with Publix and then picked up Costco. The Costco sales started small, but after about five years, they ended up being big with us. They gave us all the northeast, the mid-Atlantic, and the southeast. I'm in about a hundred and fifty stores from Maine to Florida to Texas. We had to give Texas up because I was running tight on clams. About three or four years ago, we gave up Publix. We were splitting the Publix business with another company owned by a good friend of ours. I told him that Costco was all we could handle and gave them the Publix business.

We are busting our buns to keep Costco happy. For Mother's Day week, we shipped out $150,000 worth of clams in three days. We only grow half of them and buy the other half from about twenty or thirty different farmers. They're a lot smaller and just farm and sell to us. We buy them, package them, and ship them out. It helps everybody in town, and that's the way it works. Britt has one of the farms. He's been growing clams for over twenty years and everything he grows we buy.

You might say that hard work is in the Solano DNA. My father is eighty-seven now, and a lot calmer, but if you go back thirty, forty years ago, he was a driver, hard-working, sixty hours a week, always at it. That was the kind of person he was. And with that, he built quite an empire over time. He is a real American success story. He came from dirt poor. Dirt poor, that's what I'd call it. He had nothing. He was successful because he wanted to be successful. He put forth everything he had to get there. He was with Sav-A-Stop for a long time and opened a few of those drug stores on the side. But I think it was the break with ICEE that propelled him.

My dad's always been driven. It probably has to do with his childhood and a burning desire to be successful and to make something of himself. He came along in a time when you could make it big if you worked hard, got some breaks, and took some risks. And it worked out for him.

The Captain Solano Clams package illustrated the Solano family's move into the aquaculture business.

Dan with his wife Patty

Dan's family at the 2019 Rotary Seafood Cookout. From left, Patty, Timothy, Dan, Joseph, Daniel, and Sarah Solano.

FIVE
Kimberly Solano's Story

My earliest memory of my father was opening oysters with him when I was about three years old. I remember I was barefoot with no shirt because I thought I was a boy, like my brothers. We were all in the barbeque house with my grandfather Daddy Pete, eating oysters. And I remember my mother walking in and screaming "Bob!" because I had an oyster knife and a glove, and I was digging at an oyster.

Dad said, "Karen, she needs to learn how to open them because she eats them faster than I can shuck them."

Mom said, "I can't believe you'd give our baby a knife."

He said, "She'll be just fine."

I remember that, and now I can shuck oysters faster than any of the guys. As I got older, I had to follow the boy's example because they were all so busy playing sports, and dad founded the ballpark and was president of the association for years. I started helping in the concession stands at the ballparks where my brothers were playing and dad was coaching. I remember giving my friends free Koolees and hot dogs, which didn't make my dad happy. Later, dad would take me to the office on Saturdays, and I'd stamp Koolee coupons and answer the phones. He sold the company when I was eleven and diversified into other businesses.

My brothers were all unbelievably talented in sports. My brother David, who passed away, still holds the batting average record for the state of Florida.

And he played with people like Darryl Strawberry. He was also awesome in basketball, but they all were good in sports. I was more into ballet, tap, and jazz back then.

I went to Bartram in Jacksonville and played fast pitch softball for a couple of years before I moved on to cheerleading. I was in the National Achievement Academy for cheerleading for three years, and was also an alternate for Swashbuckling, the Tampa Bay Buccaneers cheerleading squad.

One of the things dad stressed to us was working hard and saving money for a rainy day. The reason we worked so hard was for the family to thrive together. We were a very water-oriented family, swimming, water skiing, and fishing.

I love to fish, but my favorite thing about fishing, being a twentieth-generation Minorcan, was throwing a cast net. Dad taught us how to throw cast nets when we were young. Every one of us can throw a cast net, and we each have our own. We all fish for mullet together, throwing the cast nets.

We grew up hearing dad's stories. That's how he would instill his values, teaching us how to be safe when you're in the woods because we're very much woods people. And we're very much into fishing, so he had shark stories. That's how he taught us to be careful and the proper way to do things. All of dad's stories are a big part of who we are.

Since I was a little girl, I have always loved serving people. My best friend had a little burger stand on the corner, and I started working with her when I was fifteen, taking orders, and even cooking. That's part of who I am. I loved working for the Village Inn Corporation because I met people every day. During that time, I got my real estate license, and, on the side, I was working with Century Twenty-One Commercial Investment Network. I wanted to be in commercial real estate. Not residential. It's hard enough to be a woman in commercial real estate, but selling houses too, no one takes you seriously, and you'll never make it into the clique. I worked hard at it, and when I retired from Village Inn, I started my real estate company. Now I'm licensed in three states, Georgia, Alabama, and Florida doing commercial and industrial real estate. But I'm selling houses to my family because all my nieces and nephews are buying homes now.

My son Rene had attended college since he was fifteen. My dad helped me raise him, and we worked hard to get him through medical school. A year before he graduated from med school, he decided he didn't want to be a doctor. He wanted to be an entrepreneur like his grandfather. His exact words were, "I can help more people as an entrepreneur like Poppa. And I don't want to be a doctor anymore."

I nearly had a heart attack, but instead of pushing him, I said. "I just want you to be happy. I'm glad you're going to make a lot of money so you can pay me back the $800,000 it took to get you through med school.

He said, "I got to pay that back?"

"Yes, you do if you don't graduate. But if you graduate in the top one percent of your class, you owe me nothing. You can run off and do whatever you want as long as you have that doctorate. I know you can always hang out your shingle if you really need to."

I didn't think he could do it. He took a two-month sabbatical in the last year of med school and started his roofing company because he said it was a recession-proof business, and then he returned to school and finished in the top one percent at USF.

Rene's company grossed like three million dollars in his first year in business. He's been going for seven years, and he's supposed to do ten million this next year. He buys real estate like crazy. He's hired a bunch of my cousins to work with him. He does a lot of charity work. He loves animals and has a three-thousand-acre farm in Alabama-Georgia combined. Now he's branched out. He has an office and warehouse in Pensacola with people working there, and his main office here in Tampa. He's a busy guy, just like his grandfather. I'm so proud of him.

My real estate company is doing so well. I'm in a place in my life where I feel very grounded, and I want to love my family and enjoy what we all have together.

Young Kimberly Solano with her big brother Brian on a cruise in 1983.

Kimberly and her son Rene.

PART SIX

Life Is a Feast

Bobby's Rules to Live by:

14. When we are young, we don't realize how short life really is. Enjoy it now, every day.

15. Money can't buy you happiness, but it does bring you a more pleasant form of misery.

ONE
Minorcan Recipes

Over 1,400 people set off for the New World in 1768, looking for a fresh start in New Smyrna Beach, Florida. They all came to be known as Minorcans since up to eighty percent were from the Island of Minorca, but the indentured servants also included Greeks, Italians, and a handful of people from France and Catalonia. They brought traditions and family recipes from their Mediterranean culture that remain with us today through spicy dishes like Minorcan oyster stew and clam chowder I grew up eating.

Arriving in Florida, the Minorcans found abundant food sources like oysters growing right offshore, easily caught gopher tortoises, and mullet. They became such good fishermen they quickly cornered the market on supplying fish to the St. Augustine townspeople after they arrived in their new home. Minorcan food is simple, seasonal, and always fresh, often based on the seafood that was in such ample supply.

Today, tourists visit St. Augustine's restaurants to sample Minorcan clam chowder and fried shrimp, but I learned how to cook growing up with Pop and Grandma. I've passed the Minorcan traditions to my family, including cooking in the Minorcan style. Here are a few of my favorite recipes. Enjoy!

Minorcan Style Meat Sauce for Spaghetti Dinner
Whenever we have a large family gathering for the holidays or extended weekends, you can be sure that we'll prepare a large pot of spaghetti for one of

our meals. But it's not served with your usual ho-hum spaghetti sauce out of a jar. Instead, our homemade savory meat sauce has everyone asking for second helpings.

Ingredients

4 pounds ground beef (you can use turkey, pork, chicken, or venison)

2 large or medium onions, diced

1 green pepper, diced

3 tablespoons olive oil

2 quarts tomato sauce (you may use tomato sauce with garlic or green peppers if you wish)

1 can diced tomatoes

1 can stewed tomatoes

1 can mushrooms

1 small or medium can or jar of green Spanish olives (dice into quarters)

2 packages McCormick Spaghetti Powder seasoning (regular or thick)

1 teaspoon salt (more are less to your taste)

1 teaspoon black pepper (more or less to your taste)

1 to two teaspoons diced fresh garlic

¾ teaspoon oregano

½ teaspoon ground cloves

½ teaspoon ground cinnamon

2 teaspoons honey or cane syrup

1 small diced green Datil pepper with seeds removed. Or the pepper or Datil pepper sauce may be added later according to individual taste

Instructions

Add the oil, diced onions, and peppers in a big pot and brown. Don't overcook or burn.

Add the beef and brown with onions and peppers. Now add diced tomatoes, stewed tomatoes, mushrooms, and olives. Stir the contents well until mixed thoroughly.

Set on medium heat, <u>but before it comes to a boil</u> add the remainder of the ingredients, stirring as you go.

Now bring it all to a boil stirring constantly for just two to three minutes. Reduce the heat and let it simmer for thirty to forty-five minutes stirring often to be sure it doesn't burn, and nothing sticks to the bottom of the pot.

Prepare your pasta as directed on the package—we use thin spaghetti, but any kind of pasta may be used. Add the meat sauce to the pasta and enjoy.

***

My daughter Kimberly is more than an ace real estate agent (Solano Realty LLC), she's also an amazing cook. Here are a couple of her favorite recipes.

Guard your front door! The aroma may bring hungry strangers — Spanish or Minorcan ghosts from the past.

Minorcan Beans

After our family has a hearty ham dinner for whatever occasion, I like to make this simple pot of beans. The night before cooking, I soak the dry beans in water. If you are short on time, then a quick soak direction is located on the bag of dried beans.

Take leftover ham bone and hock and cover with water in a stock pot and bring to boil.

Season water generously with the following:

2 teaspoons of ground cloves

1 teaspoon of ground coriander

2 tablespoons of dried oregano

5 cloves of garlic peeled and smashed or minced

Salt to taste (keep in mind the ham is salty)

Pepper to taste (I use a ton)

3-5 bay leaves

Return to boil then reduce to rapid simmer

Prep your vegetables:

4 chopped medium sized Vidalia onions

1 chopped large bell pepper (pick your favorite color and flavor)

When the ham falls off soup bone after a couple hours of simmering, discard skin, grizzle and bones.

Bring back to boil then reduce to rapid simmer and add your chopped veggies.

Time to add your soaked beans. Strain your soaking water off the beans first.

Bring back to boil and then reduce to low simmer and cook uncovered till beans soften and shell of bean splits stirring frequently so beans do not burn to bottom of stock pot. We eat our beans soupy, but most people like them thicker. If you find your beans are too soupy after you have cooked them to desired softness and consistency, then add a half a cup of self-rising corn meal and cook for another 20-30 minutes until thick.

As you can see this recipe is a full afternoon of fun, so I suggest you use a large ham and a couple pounds of beans. They freeze wonderfully for a quick meal any day of the week.

Serving Suggestion:

A dab of Datil pepper or Datil pepper vinegar makes them Minorcan.

Fresh raw chopped Vidalia and your favorite cornbread or crusty French bread.

Enjoy from my family to yours.

***

Minorcan Corn Bread

Ingredients
1-1/2 cups of self-rising white or yellow cornmeal

1 cup of sour cream

2 eggs

1 cup of milk

1 cup of corn or 1 cup of cream corn

1 large jalapeno or 2 small jalapenos chopped and seeded

1/2 fresh Datil pepper finely minced or sliced. REMOVE SEEDS

salt and pepper to taste

Preheat the oven to 450 degrees.

Oil or butter cast iron skillet and place in 450-degree oven for 5-10 minutes until pan is smoking hot. Please be careful. Mix ingredients well and pour into hot skillet. It should sizzle.

Bake for 30 minutes or until golden brown and toothpick comes away clean. Serve hot with a drizzle of honey or a dab of butter.

***

Minorcan Clam Chowder
One of everyone's favorite Minorcan recipes is clam chowder. Unlike the traditional clam chowder, which is made with milk and cream, Minorcan Clam Chowder is red and made with tomato paste and spicy but sweet Datil peppers, among many other ingredients. The following recipe is borrowed from the popular Old City restaurant, the St. Augustine Seafood Company.

Ingredients

2 dozen Florida clams*

4 ounces salt pork or bacon

1 datil pepper, minced use half a pepper if you're heat shy

1 medium onion, diced

1 green bell pepper, diced

2 medium carrots, diced

1 cup small red potatoes, peeled and diced

1 15-ounce can chopped tomatoes

3 tablespoons tomato paste

1 teaspoon fresh garlic, minced (1-2 cloves)

1 teaspoon oregano

1 teaspoon rosemary

1 teaspoon thyme

1 teaspoon salt

3 bay leaves

1 eight-ounce bottle clam juice

2 cups fish stock

Instructions

Take 4 ounces of salt pork and cut into small pieces. If using bacon, cut crosswise into 1/2-inch pieces. Place in a soup pot and cook for 10 minutes. When the salt pork (or bacon) is browned, remove and place on a paper towel, leaving the rendered fat in the pot. Add the diced onion, green pepper, and carrots to the rendered fat and cook 5-10 minutes until the onions are translucent.

Stir in one 15-ounce can of chopped tomatoes, 3 tablespoons of tomato paste, all the seasonings (use fresh or dried) and bay leaves. Add one minced Datil pepper or 2-3 teaspoons of Datil hot sauce (to taste).

Next, add the 8-ounce bottle of clam juice and 2 cups of fish stock. Simmer on low heat for 1 hour.

Meanwhile, place the 2 dozen fresh clams in a colander in the sink. Lightly scrub the outside of the clams and rinse to remove any dirt or sand. Place the clams in a large pan over medium-high heat with 1/3 cup of water. Cover the pan and cook the clams for approximately 10 minutes until the clams open. Remove from stove.

Using a slotted spoon, place the clams in a colander, let drain. Throw away any unopened clams. When the clams cool, remove the meat from the shells. Chop the clam meat into bite-size pieces. Set aside. Discard clam shells.

Next, add one cup of the diced potatoes to the soup and cook approximately 20 minutes or until the potatoes are tender, but not mushy. Add the chopped clams and cooked salt pork. Cook just long enough for the clams and pork to be heated through - approx. 5 minutes. Taste and adjust seasonings if necessary. This soup tastes even better the next day because the flavors have had more time to meld.

*Recipe Notes

If you are using canned minced clams, drain the clams, retaining the juice to use instead of the bottled clam juice. You'll have about 1 cup of clam juice from two 6.5-ounce cans of clams.

AFTERWORD

This book has been a longtime work in progress. Writing about my life was like opening the door to my memory vault and letting the memories flood over me. Just thinking about my friends and family and how they assisted me in my journey through life was almost overwhelming.

After reading *The Last Beach Boy,* you know I came from humble beginnings. I didn't have a college degree, but I believe in the value of education and how it can help people meet their goals. I may have lacked an advanced academic education, but my practical experience forged the way toward a better future for my family and me.

Who knows how my life might have been different if I'd gone to college or made other choices along the way? Little decisions and chance encounters impact our lives. A left turn instead of a right turn leads to a different destination. Walking on the beach at sunset instead of sunrise or striking up a conversation with a stranger might alter the course of your life.

What if my friend Jim Minton had never called me about the Sav-A-Stop job? Would I have spent years digging ditches for the Jacksonville Beach Sewer Department? Or if I hadn't seen that first ICEE machine in Pensacola? How different would my life be today?

We don't think about those things until much later in life. Did I make mistakes along the way? Sure, but if you asked me if I'd change anything and possibly alter my future, I'd first consider how everything turned out with my family and the wonderful friends I made along the way.

My first marriage produced some beautiful children. I'm so proud of them and love them with all my heart. Without my second marriage, I wouldn't have my wonderful daughter Kimberly. So, I'd have to say I wouldn't change a thing.

Life is not fair. Some people suffer more than others. Some people have so much empathy they hurt when other people are injured. Other folks, unfortunately, are users. They are wrapped up in themselves and don't care how their words and actions affect others. I've found my peace in my religion. If a person doesn't believe in God, what do they believe?

As parents, we should heed the words of the great teachers and philosophers and teach our children well. Use the proper discipline and be a good role model, and they'll grow up knowing you love them. Although some may stray, they'll usually return to the right path because you instilled the proper family values in them.

As this final chapter ends, I thank a father I hardly knew, my mother for her love and support, and my sister Joyce, who was always the smartest person in our family. Special thanks to my loving Grandma and Pop, who taught me about life.

Growing up on the beach, watching the waves and the changing tides taught me many lessons. I learned to be strong yet calm. That you can't learn to swim in shallow waters—you have to jump in, even if it's over your head, and go with the current. There's a time to tread water and a time to swim like hell. Most of all, I learned that the sun does come up every morning, and there's always time for a fresh start and new opportunities.

This Beach Boy had a charmed life, and like scoring a buzzer-beater during our championship season, there is no better feeling than knowing you went out a winner. And here are my last words of advice from this old Beach Boy to the younger folks reading this book:

Finish school, then get out and find a job, any job, but work to be the best at your job. That action will move you forward in every step of your working life. While you're earning money, be sure to save and invest. Above

all, stick with your family through thick and thin. Honor your mother and father. Maybe they were not perfect, but without them you wouldn't be here!

Give back to good causes to help others and give a dollar now and then to that homeless person on the street corner. Helping others helps you understand how blessed you really are. Believe me, you will remember these good deeds, and they'll put a smile on your face when your time is up.

Here's to my wonderful family and great friends from my school days and friends I have had the privilege to meet and work with, and to everyone who reads my book.

May the road rise to meet you.
May the wind be always at your back.
May the sun shine warm on your face,
the rains fall soft upon your fields and until we meet again,
may God hold you in the palm of his hand forever.

Bobby Solano

About The Co-Author

Victor DiGenti (aka Parker Francis) writes both fiction and non-fiction. As an award-winning author he's written six novels and a collection of short stories. As a biographer/ghostwriter/book doctor/publisher he helps individuals turn their memories into literary legacies. He's collaborated to write books for World War II veterans, and others who have led fascinating lives and found success in diverse professional fields ranging from real estate, economics, music, and psychology. Visit him at www.parkerfrancis.com.